THE PENNSYLVANIA STATE UNIVERSITY STUDIES NO. 21

THE ATTITUDE OF BUSINESS TOWARD AMERICAN FOREIGN POLICY, 1900-1916

by HERBERT ERSHKOWITZ

THE PENNSYLVANIA STATE UNIVERSITY
University Park, Pennsylvania

PREFACE

The foreign policy of the United States is not created in a vacuum but is the product of both domestic and external pressures. Most historical studies of American diplomacy have been concerned primarily with the response of American statesmen to external events. The traditionalist in history is generally preoccupied with diplomatic maneuvers, international conferences, and ratification of treaties. In adopting this frame of reference, the part which American opinion has exercised in the formation of foreign policy has generally been neglected. Yet in a sense that is true in no other nation, American diplomatic action has been determined by the people.

The period 1900-1916 was very important in that it laid a very real foundation for the twentieth century foreign policy of the United States. My purpose in undertaking this study of the attitudes of one segment of opinion is to determine what was the mood of the American people as the United States moved towards a greater role in world affairs. I have studied organized business in this essay because in 1900 it was the most powerful interest group in American society. Moreover, the various segments of the business community through their associations and trade journals were able to vocalize their attitudes on foreign policy in a much more lucid manner than any other group. This does not mean that the other segments of American public opinion should be slighted. A more complete understanding of

American foreign policy in the twentieth century is dependent upon studies of labor, the various ethnic groups, and the much misunderstood agricultural interests. I hope this volume will provide a stimulus for other such studies.

I wish to acknowledge special indebtedness to Professor Vincent P. Carosso who read this manuscript and was most generous in offering advice, assistance, and encouragement.

Temple University   *Herbert Ershkowitz*
October, 1966

CONTENTS

1 THE THESIS OF OVERPRODUCTION

During the nineteenth century, while the remainder of the nation was apathetic toward foreign affairs, the American businessman maintained a constant interest in the world beyond his shores. His commercial brand of internationalism, created by a desire for world markets, brought him into contact with Europe, Asia, and South America. Eventually, his influence upon public policy was to cause the United States to reverse its traditional isolationism. The business community became especially interested in international affairs during the late 1890's and early 1900's because of the threat of overproduction.

Men such as William Dodsworth, Brooks Adams, and Charles Conant sought to provide an answer to the problems posed by the rapid development of industry during the second half of the nineteenth century.[1] According to Dodsworth, the world's major industrial countries, Germany, England, and the United States, were producing more goods than they could consume.[2] While the exports of the eight major industrial nations had quadrupled during the last fifty years, the populations of these nations had increased only approximately one-third. The conclusion he drew was that each of these nations had an increasing surplus of goods that could not be consumed at home and which had to be exported. Dodsworth saw in the falling price level a further indication that this was true. From 1874-1896, retail prices had fallen thirty-six per cent.

1

Since falling prices had made entrance into new ventures unprofitable, Charles Conant found that in addition to an overproduction of goods, there was also a surplus of capital caused by a lessening domestic demand. This lessening demand for capital led to a decline in the interest rate, which had fallen from 4.17 to 2.5 per cent.[3]

J. M. Thompson of the New England Cotton Manufacturers' Association attributed overproduction of goods, and the consequential decline in prices and interest rates, to new machines and other labor-saving devices.[4] Dodsworth similarly blamed steam power for the increased production. Acceleration of the tendency to overproduce had become more marked because of the change in the products manufactured. At first, concentration centered on building plants. Now that these were relatively complete, the emphasis had shifted to consumer goods.[5]

This overextension of the industrial plant, according to Dodsworth, threatened capitalism. In order to halt falling prices, movements to by-pass the natural laws of competition and to form monopolies had arisen. "But in spite of these artificial restraints, supply still kept getting ahead of demand and prices continued to decline."[6] Dodsworth warned that since there was an increase in the number of people dependent on industrial production, overproduction would produce a national disaster. He pessimistically predicted:

> If relief is not forthcoming, a stage of great industrial collapse, attended with the agitation of equally grave political issues, becomes only too probable, and the energies of our society — five millions of producers — may have to be restrained.[7]

To prevent the dissolution of society and the economic chaos which would result from the closing of the industrial plant because of overproduction, Conant offered these alternate solutions: (1) A planned socialistic economy. (2) Creation of new demands at home through waste and war. (3) The sale of surplus goods to countries not as yet enjoying modern means of production.[8]

At that time the first two suggestions were unacceptable to the United States. The only hope for business seemed to lie in the third proposal. Yet, acceptance of the second suggestion might have ended overproduction without the dangers of encountering complications on an international scale. Keynes, many years later, suggested that overproduction could be eliminated by increasing home consumption. Overproduction existed

2

because business denied to the worker the very goods he produced. Instead of raising the general American standard of living, businessmen tried to find buyers in the countries of the world where poverty was even more prevalent than in the United States.

The president of the National Association of Manufacturers agreed with the philosophers of overproduction when he said: "American manufacturers no longer measure their productive capacity by the consuming power of their home markets; for the world is their market and all the people of the earth are their customers."[9]

Edward Atkinson, writing in the *North American Review,* stated: "The main object of the people of the United States now is to find a market for their surplus products of the field, the factory, the mine and the workshop."[10]

But where could American trade be directed? Europe, consisting largely of manufacturing nations, was experiencing the same problems as the United States. This left only the underdeveloped regions of the world, such as the Orient or South America, open to American export trade.

China, with four hundred million potential customers, appeared to be the ideal market for industry to dispose of its surplus. Some businessmen even calculated how much of their products would be sold if each Chinese bought only a small quantity. One textile journal, for example, estimated that America would export six hundred thirty-four million dollars worth of cotton yarn if the average Chinese could be made to consume only one half the amount used by the average American.[11] Such an expansion of the China trade alone would mean a doubling of cotton manufacturing facilities.

These speculations as to what the Chinese market would be in the future led a group of businessmen to form the American Asiatic Society in 1898. Composed of a membership which read like a *Who's Who* in American business, the Society campaigned through its organ, *Asia,* for a greater business and governmental interest in China. In one of its first issues, *Asia* noted that since China was one of the most promising fields for American commerce, American businessmen could not afford to disregard political rivalries there as long as they hoped to become competitors in the world-wide struggle for trade.[12]

The textile interests, which had already entered the Chinese market, considered further exports as a guarantee of future prosperity. Consequently, at the 1901 meeting of the New

3

England Cotton Manufacturers, nearly half of the speakers discussed ways of maintaining and broadening sales of textiles in the Orient. Because of this special interest in the Chinese market, the textile manufacturers were among the leaders in advocating an advanced Far Eastern policy. An analysis of the membership of the American Asiatic Society reveals a preponderance of textile men. Moreover, at least one-half of the advertising in *Asia* was purchased by the same manufacturers.[13] Since most American cotton was sold in Manchuria, American fears of Russian encroachment played a significant role in the announcement of the Open Door Policy. Apprehensions over the loss of this textile market cannot be overestimated.

Business interest in the Orient was greatly stimulated by the Spanish American War. Although the original business attitude on American expansion was unfavorable, the possibility of an American base in the Philippines, so close to the China mainland, excited businessmen.[14] They envisioned American trade expansion through these islands. In fact, many businessmen predicted that Manila would soon rival Singapore and Hong Kong as a Far Eastern trading center, thus placing the United States on a par with England in sharing the Chinese market.

The president of the National Association of Manufacturers in 1903 viewed the battle of Manila Bay as "a battle which, perhaps did more toward making this nation a great maritime and commercial power than many are ready to acknowledge."[15] The prospects of an American empire, even if it did lay the basis for an expansion of trade in the Far East, did not win universal business approval. Andrew Carnegie was a most vocal opponent of McKinley's expansionist policy, arguing that the suppression of the Philippines did much to lessen our democracy while it did little to advance our commercial interests. Carnegie had already begun his campaign for world peace. Realizing the connection between imperialism and war, Carnegie was opposed to all imperialism, be it that of the British in South Africa or that of the United States in the Philippines.[16]

Besides Carnegie, there were other businessmen who felt that America's future trade did not depend on China. They argued that China, in its great poverty, could not consume the surplus goods of the United States.[17] Even four hundred million persons could not become customers if they did not have something to trade. Essentially, it was this group of business prognosticators who in time proved to be correct. No matter how much American business may have dreamed of a large Chinese market,

4

it never materialized. By the middle 1920's, there was still talk of future Chinese trade. The reasons the Chinese market never did materialize was pointed out as early as 1900. The Chinese population was just too poor to buy in the world market, and the government too unstable to exercise any control to bring about any internal change. Yet, this myth of the Chinese market was to play as important a role in the shaping of our foreign policy as the theory of overproduction.

As a substitute for a nonexistent Chinese market, the suggestion was made that business look to other world markets to dispose of its surpluses. One possibility was an increase in trade with Europe.[18] That continent was one of the United States' best customers and had the money and products with which to trade with us. The *United States Investor* considered Latin America, which had been neglected by business, a better market than China.[19] The United States had cultural ties and reasonably friendly relations with Latin America. These conditions contrasted markedly with the United States' relationship to China.

Those businessmen who subscribed to the thesis of overproduction and to the belief that American trade expansion must come in China thought that they were in the midst of a trade war. This idea arose because all the industrial nations had experienced difficulty in disposing of unwanted surpluses. Since the major battle of this trade war came in the Orient, America's position there had to be strengthened. John Barrett, former Minister to Siam and a member of the American Asiatic Society, offered the following program: (1) The construction of a Central American Canal. (2) The laying of the Pacific cable. (3) The development of American shipping in the Pacific. (4) The raising of standards in the diplomatic and consular services.[20]

The Southern Cotton Spinners Association agreed with Barrett's suggestions but urged an increase in the size of the Navy so that it could provide protection for American shipping.[21] At the same time, the National Association of Manufacturers pleaded for a reciprocal trade program, a suggestion which did not please many of its members.[22]

Of the methods mentioned, business most desired the building of an inter-oceanic canal. Warner Miller, an American consul to China, thought that such a canal would be as advantageous to the United States in exploiting the Far East as the opening of the Suez Canal had been to Europe in exploiting the Orient.

5

Before 1900, when America's surplus was primarily agricultural, she was not in competition with Europe and did not need a quick cheap method of reaching the Far East. Now, however, to eliminate America's industrial surplus, Miller felt that the United States needed the

> more than 500 million people who live on its [the Pacific] borders. . . . China is about to be opened to the commerce of the world. . . . If we are to have our own fair share, we must be prepared to step in and establish our trade in the country upon terms which will enable us to compete with the manufacturers of Europe.[23]

A quick crossing of the isthmus would relieve the American shipper of the disadvantages of going through the Suez Canal. American products traveled from New York to Shanghai by a route four thousand miles longer than a comparable shipment from Liverpool; whereas, through an inter-oceanic canal, America would have the advantage. Yokahoma would be 1803 miles closer to the eastern shore of the United States than it was to England.[24]

Not only was the canal vital to the development of American trade in the Orient, but is was also necessary to build up a Central and South American market. The building of a canal would end the thriving business which the English and Germans were doing there. *Iron Age* felt that a direct route to the west coast of South and Central America would at least double the amount of merchandise Latin America imported from the United States.[25] There was even some indication that the building of a canal would encourage the merchants of Central America to move toward annexation with the United States.[26]

Although considerable unanimity existed among business interests on the desirability of building a canal, their harmony did not extend to the questions raised by the Hay-Pauncefote Treaty, namely, the relationship between the government and the canal, and whether the canal should be neutral in time of war. Opposition to the treaty came from many sources, among them the *Philadelphia Manufacturer*. The editors wrote that the canal should be conducted on business principles, like the Suez Canal. It should be neutral territory, free to all comers who will pay for passing through it. The aid which the United States Government gives to this enterprise should be the kind England gives to the Suez Canal.[27] The Iron and Steel Association also voiced its opposition to the treaty. The Association thought that the clause of the treaty which guaranteed the neutrality of the canal

6

would prevent the United States from fortifying the approaches by water. The compact would put the United States at more of a disadvantage than it would any other power. That section "practically vetoes the principle of governmental control stated in the first clause of the treaty."[28]

In response to that criticism, the Senate revised the Hay-Pauncefote Treaty, removing the neutrality provision. The *Commercial and Financial Chronicle* reacted unfavorably to this change. The periodical warned that the new treaty might lead to the completion of a competitive Central American Canal, making the American canal unprofitable.[29]

When the Hay-Herran Treaty was rejected by the Colombian Senate, President Theodore Roosevelt sent the United States Navy to Panama to aid the revolution which had broken out there. An editorial in the *Commercial and Financial Chronicle* was representative of the almost unanimous business approval of the President's action. The editorial justified this naval intervention for these reasons: (1) The past commitments of the United States under the treaty with Colombia to maintain free and uninterrupted transit across the Isthmus in times of internal instability. (2) The dishonorable action of the Colombian Senate in rejecting the treaty. (3) The misrule of Colombia in Panama which had produced this internal revolution.[30]

The rebuilding of the American merchant fleet, business felt, was secondary in importance as a means of gaining trade. The interest in the project is illustrated by a statement from *Iron Age*: "The business world is thoroughly alive and in hearty accord on the general question that the next great achievement before our people is to recover that supremacy on the seas which once we held."[31]

The basis for this interest was the belief that trade followed lines of transportation. Since the American carrying trade was dependent on European rivals, the United States was completely at their mercy. Nationals of England and Germany chose the routes that American goods were to follow, and the ports at which they were to be deposited. This resulted in the blocking off of possible lucrative markets. For example, in many parts of South America it was easier to receive mail and cargo from Germany than from the eastern coast of the United States. With our own fleet, a direct link with South America would be established. In addition, America would be the master of Oriental trade. *Iron Age* used the rise of German commerce as an example for the United States to follow.[32] German influence in

7

Latin America dated only from the development of a merchant marine. Germany, not being dependent on foreign shipping, directed her goods to Latin America, which was ripe for exploitation.

At its annual convention, the National Association of Manufacturers, which constituted the most powerful pressure group in favor of the rebuilding of the American merchant marine, resolved:

> That the National Association of Manufacturers, mindful of these great advantages to the nation for the transportation of American products, mails, imports and passengers, under our flag . . . demand of Congress the enactment of suitable laws for the restoration of an American merchant marine to make us independent in time of peace and war.[33]

How was the merchant marine, which in 1901 carried only nine per cent of America's overseas trade, to be restored to its former position? There was a great divergence of opinion on this point. Faced by attacks from socialists and other radical groups, a large segment of business had rallied to the defense of *laissez-faire*. These opponents of socialism felt they could not now advocate government aid for business. The *Journal of Commerce* wrote: "It is not sound policy to take out of the treasury funds raised by taxation and hand them over to persons engaged in a private business to cover their loss."[34] This view was neither consistent with our past history, nor with the aid business had already received from government in the form of tariff protection and grants to railroads.

Realizing that a governmental subsidy to business would be no innovation, the National Board of Trade at its annual convention advocated a federal allotment to American ships of five thousand tons or over.[35] Such a departure from *laissez-faire* was defended on the grounds that it was the only way for the United States to compete with European lines already subsidized by their governments and to overcome the higher costs of American labor. If a similar demand for a subsidy had been made by a farm or by a labor group, business would have attacked the plan as a socialistic innovation. The National Board of Trade, as well as most other business groups, regarded aid to business as the best means of promoting the nation's welfare.

The leading exponent of shipping subsidies was the American Iron and Steel Association. Individual business groups and industries viewed American foreign policy as it suited their own

8

special interests. Since the iron and steel industry benefited from shipping subsidies, it worked for them. The contracts for building a merchant marine would go to this industry. It concealed its motives behind an idea which seemed to be advantageous to the nation. The industry stated in its bulletin:

> Better, far better, than the best reciprocity treaty that could be devised would be the adoption of a liberal policy of government subsidies which would give us steamship lines carrying the American flag and American goods to all parts of the world.[36]

To further American expansion into the Far East, the American Association of China petitioned Congress to improve the Consular Service.[37] To support this stand, the National Association of Manufacturers backed the Lodge bill.[38] This measure, devised by Henry Cabot Lodge, one of the staunchest Senate supporters of business, provided for the creation of a consular service based on the merit system, taking it out of politics and applying to it sound business methods.

Business' attitude on the inter-oceanic canal, on the rebuilding of the American Navy, and on the other measures just cited was directed by its belief that America was producing too much merchandise to be consumed at home. Although business may have presented other arguments, it viewed the foreign policy of the nation just as it would a sales campaign. The purpose of the government, according to this philosophy, was to increase trade possibilities.

2 | THE OPEN DOOR AND AFTERWARDS

During the first ten years of the twentieth century, commercial and financial interest in foreign affairs was focused on the Far East. Business feared that the United States might lose valuable outlets for its surpluses if the Far East was closed by one of America's competitors. Because the American government was sympathetic to the desire of industry for a market in the Orient, the United States' aim in foreign policy was to further this end. William Phillips, an Assistant Secretary of State, in President Taft's administration revealed the extent of this commitment. This official declared that the government was in favor of a general extension of its influence in China, "so that when the commercial interests and exporters of the United States turn their attention more and more vigorously toward securing the markets of the Orient, they will find those of China open to their products and the Chinese public favorably disposed to American enterprise."[1]

In order to keep China open to American trade, it was necessary for the United States to take a positive stand against the European countries that were about to annex parts of the Chinese Empire. Such annexations would have probably resulted in an exclusion of American trade from China.[2] Since the greater part of the American trade to China went to the Manchurian provinces, business was primarily concerned with Russian activities there. Russian influence had been extended to Port Arthur and then to Tailieman, the chief entry port for American goods into Manchuria. If Russia did exclude American goods from this lucrative market, the economy of the American South would have been seriously affected, because one-half of all Southern cotton cloth exported went to this Chinese province. Businessmen from other parts of the United States were concerned that England, France, and Germany would follow Russia's precedent by taking control of other parts of China. The *United States Investor* predicted that America would lose the Chinese market before it was ready to dominate it. Since the loss of China would be a national as well as a commercial disaster, business urged that no policy be neglected which the American government found necessary in order to guarantee equal rights to everyone in China.[3] Consequently, a speaker at the New England Cotton Manufacturer's Convention called upon the government to see that American interests in northern China were fully protected. He wanted assurances that if Russia gained control over this territory American trade would continue as in the past.

Since the government was committed to a policy of advancing American trade in the Orient, the State Department acted to prevent American commercial exclusion from China. In the Open Door Notes of 1899, John Hay first stated the American position that spheres of influence should not interfere with the collection of the Chinese tariff — or discriminate against the goods of other nations. Although they supported the position taken by John Hay, commercial leaders expressed the view that the Secretary of State should have taken a stronger stand. Since spheres of influence must lead to a division of China by the European nations and to the complete exclusion of American trade from China, business warned that only the maintenance of the territorial integrity of China would guarantee accessibility for all nations.[5] If Chinese integrity were left undisturbed, *Iron Age* wrote, American goods would defeat competition because whenever American products vied with European commodities in Asia America was supreme.[6] John Barrett also viewed the Open Door Policy as the cornerstone of America's economic welfare, but he held that the great trade possibilities of the United States in China would be forfeited if Chinese territorial integrity were not preserved. Barrett thought that if Chinese integrity wasn't maintained we might as well allow Germany to take over the Philippines, ask England to build the canal, and Japan to lay her own cable.[7]

John Hay's response to this commercial criticism was the

second Open Door Note. Circulated during the Boxer Rebellion, Hay's note urged the preservation of China's territorial and administrative integrity. Hay thereby laid the foundation of twentieth century American Far Eastern foreign policy. The Secretary of State's policy won the universal acclaim of American commerce. The *Commercial and Financial Chronicle,* for example, called Hay a great foreign minister whose policies had charted a new path to greatness in American foreign affairs.[8]

Though business realized that the Open Door was a commercial policy, many statesmen later viewed it as a moral end in itself. Moreover, when the original purpose of this policy had passed into obscurity, it became as sacroscant as the Monroe Doctrine. John Foord, secretary of the American Asiatic Association, in answering critics of Hay's policy claimed that the two doctrines were interdependent. The Monroe Doctrine was simply a declaration of the Open Door for this continent.[9] This interpretation of the Secretary's policy was to play great havoc with later American-Far Eastern relations.[10] Furthermore, one by-product of the Open Door Policy was the idea that the success of this policy depended on a close American cooperation with the Anglo-Japanese alliance. Because both the United States and Great Britain had to protect their national outlets or be suffocated, they had the largest stake in the Orient. Consequently, the president of the American-Asiatic Association wrote: "Whatever we do or advocate . . . it should . . . be strenuously in the direction of helping our British brethren in their noble work of keeping or making the 'open door' for Asiatic commerce."[11]

The most serious threat to Chinese integrity occurred during the Boxer Rebellion. The Boxers did considerable damage to foreign property in 1900. The inability of the Chinese government to suppress the rebellion raised the question of possible intervention by the Great Powers. Business expressed the fear that intervention would give Russia, France, and Germany an opportunity to divide up China. The reason these nations were a threat to Chinese territorial integrity, according to the *American Banker,* was "Neither Russia, France, nor Germany wants freedom of trade in China since both the United States and Great Britain would then be practically in exclusive possession of the field with their immense resources of skill and capital." The writer of the same editorial expressed the belief that Russia was the greatest threat to China because it might disregard the other powers and act on its own initiative.[12]

The United States government became involved in the rebellion when the Boxers destroyed American as well as European business property. Since it was the duty of the government to protect American enterprises abroad, the United States had the responsibility of bringing this disorder to a close, if China could not; but the fulfillment of this obligation could have led to serious consequences. If the United States were to support international intervention in China, could it then prevent the dividing up of Chinese territory by the invading nations? The business press gave this problem comprehensive coverage. For example, the *American Banker* was opposed to the United States' restoring order in the Empire by acting in concert with other nations, because, "it may lead to an attack on the final question involving the control of Chinese territory, from which it might be impossible to withdraw without great injury to our economic interest there."[13] The opposing business view was that the government had an obligation to intervene in China in order to rescue businessmen who were rightly in China and entitled to protection under existing treaties.[14]

Secretary of State Hay acted in a manner which most business leaders supported. In conjunction with the other besieged powers, Hay sent a force of United States Marines to suppress the Boxers. Meanwhile, he had made the announcement that the United States did not want to see the territory of China divided among the powers. This pronouncement, which became the second part of the Open Door Policy was greeted with enthusiasm by businessmen. They also were quite happy with the manner in which Hay had managed to settle the dilemma of protecting American property in China while preventing the dissolution of the Empire.[15] The American Asiatic Association predicted that the suppression of the Boxers would have a beneficial effect on the Chinese officials. As a consequence of the European and American intervention, the Peking government, which had been notorious in its violations of treaties, would realize it must fulfill its international obligations.[16] John Barrett also believed that the suppression of the Boxers had increased United States prestige in China. Because the United States had acted to prevent the destruction of its integrity, China realized that the United States was not using its military power or its commerce to foster territorial expansion.[17] In contrast to these observations, the *American Banker* feared that the question of Chinese unity was yet unsettled. The periodical was dissatisfied with the large idemnity China had to pay for damages resulting from the Boxer Rebellion. The *American Banker* felt that the large idemnity would lead to Chinese resistance which would give the European powers a chance to receive a settlement in land. Furthermore, the possibility existed that the presence of foreign troops on Chinese soil would lead to a second uprising.[18]

Hay's Open Door Policy did not end the threat to China's territorial unity. Its greatest enemy was Russia, a country with whom the United States maintained a tradition of friendship. American business having participated in Russia's growth by supplying engineers and equipment for the building of the Trans-Siberian Railroad, businessmen shared this sympathy. The metal industry, which had profited the most by the Russian railroad, was loudest in its praise of the Russian achievements. *Iron Age* wrote that the opening of the railroad would provide the widest possible commercial opportunities for Americans. The opening of new Russian areas by the railroad would increase its need for American engineers, manufacturing equipment, and ships.[19]

Russia, in the course of extending to the Pacific, had overflowed its boundaries into Manchuria. Consequently, it was this pressure on the northern provinces of China which caused Hay to issue the Open Door notes. By 1903 Russia's intrusion into Manchuria had threatened the Open Door principle and American commerce. Russia in that year closed the port of Harbin to other nations because she said that the city was an important rail center. The result of this action was a decline in the number of Manchurian purchases of American kerosene.

Business responded by turning against its long-time Russian friend. The *Commercial and Financial Chronicle* warned Russia that the United States would not tolerate the destruction of Chinese integrity.[20] The American Asiatic Association wrote that Russia, as a nation without scruples or honesty, could no longer depend upon American support as one of the assets of its diplomacy.[21] One financier even went to great pains to prove that Russo-American friendship was based on an historical fallacy. He discounted the idea that a Russian threat during the Civil War had prevented England from entering the war on the side of the Confederacy. Since Russia had not provided the Union with a great deal of aid during the conflict, the United States did not owe her anything.[22]

In contrast to its hostile attitude toward Russia, business showed a marked sympathy toward Japan, which was praised because of her ability to adapt herself to western culture. Jacob

14

Schiff, a partner in Kuhn, Loeb and Company, was impressed by the fairness of the Japanese position in the Orient. He believed that the Russian seizure of Lio-Tung, after Japan's exclusion from this peninsula by the great powers was unwarranted and that it was a threat to Japanese security.[23] While Russian activity in Manchuria was condemned as the great threat to the Open Door, Japanese opposition to Russia's encroachment there was greeted by business as a defense of civilization. Since the European countries had allowed Russia to extend her control over Manchuria without interference, the *Financial and Commercial Chronicle* thought that Japan, as the only country willing to defend Chinese unity, was justified in using force against Russia.[24] Expressing a similar point of view, *American Industries* wrote that though a Russian domination of Manchuria would lead to the exclusion of all American goods, there was little to fear from Japan, a country that always maintained the Open Door. Thus, by 1904, business had come to the defense of the Japanese position in Manchuria as opposed to the Russian position.[25]

Consequently, when the Russo-Japanese War broke out, business had a considerable interest in it. The war began when Japanese gunboats launched a surprise attack on Russian ships at Port Arthur. This assault followed a breakdown in negotiations between the two powers over Manchuria and Korea. Realizing that the outcome of this conflict would determine America's commercial future in the Orient, business leaders indicated great concern over the result. They also watched the course of the war in fear that the localized fighting in Manchuria would spread into a world-wide conflict. Moreover, because American financial and industrial leaders supplied many of the weapons and much of the capital to both sides, they had a monetary interest in the war.

This sympathetic business attitude towards Japan continued throughout the war. Because of its surprise attack on Russia, Japan at the outset of the war had lost much of the support of non-business opinion. However, the *Commercial and Financial Chronicle* defended the attack as Japan's only alternative to a complete submission to Russia.

> Russia did not propose to make any serious concessions. . . . At the start the Russian government assumed towards Japan a tone that might fairly be described as arrogant. . . . It is now admitted by the Russian government itself that it had no purpose of making serious concessions.[26]

15

John Foord said that it was to America's advantage as the greatest power in the Pacific to see that neither Germany nor Russia dominates Asia. Consequently, America must sympathize with Japan in her efforts to keep Russia out of the Chinese provinces and Korea.[27] The *American Banker* also placed the whole blame for the war on Russia. The Czar, this financial journal pointed out, had prolonged the negotiations purposely in order to move his armies and navies. Japan, however, was not deceived by Russia's treacherous diplomacy. If Russia had not insisted on continuing her aggression in China, the war could have been prevented.[28] One business leader wrote that nothing Russia could say would make the American people believe that a Russian success in the war would mean any advantages for the United States. He hoped that Russia would be forced by the war to abandon the monopoly she had in Manchuria. "Then the now idle and ruined factories built there by Americans could be turned to profitable account again."[29] Japan, by its surprise attack, had not lost any American business support. On the contrary, business was convinced that a victory by Japan would restore the Manchurian trade that was being destroyed by Russia.

Russia tried to overcome the pro-Japanese orientation of American public opinion by promoting itself as the defender of civilization against the threat of the "yellow peril." This Russian attempt to gain America's sympathy was rejected by business. It expressed the opinion that Japanese domination over Asia was preferable to Russian control because Japan would be a profitable associate in developing Far Eastern markets.[30] Besides, *American Industries* editorialized, there was little ground for apprehension that Japan would dominate the markets of Manchuria, since the Japanese could not compete with Western nations in cheapness of goods.[31]

One index of the favorable financial attitude towards Japan was the relative ease with which she secured loans from American capitalists. When American money lenders were first approached by Baron Takahashi, the Japanese financial representative, the prospects for securing a loan did not seem very hopeful. Nevertheless, Jacob Schiff, who had already displayed sympathy toward Japan, collaborated with Takahashi in having Japanese war bonds issued through Kuhn, Loeb, and Company. United States financiers subscribed to one half of the ten million pound bond issue; the other half was sold in London.[32] Japan considered the loan a sign that British and American businessmen were favorable to the Japanese cause. The validity of this belief can be substantiated by the fact that the loan to Japan was made at a time when foreign investments were not yet a part of American high finance. That Schiff and his associates were able to raise two more loans — the last one on very favorable terms to Japan — indicates still further that many financiers were favorably disposed to the Japanese cause. These loans were very important to the Japanese cause, since German and French hostility prevented Japan from selling bonds in these two countries. It has been estimated that one-fifth of the entire sum spent on Japanese military activities during the Russo-Japanese War was lent by the United States.[33]

Although business gave a great deal of support to Japan, there were many businessmen who felt that the war was of no concern to America as long as United States commerce was not harmed by the conflict. The *Wall Street Journal* discounted the idea that Japan was fighting for either its own liberty or the liberty of China. Instead, this eminent financial paper cautioned, this was

> essentially a commercial war. Moreover it is to be noted that the two nations [are] contending over the occupation of territory which in reality does not belong to them. They are in the position of two dogs which are struggling over a bone belonging to a harmless and unbelligerent cat. . . . The attitude of John Hay and the United States has rightly been . . . let Russia and Japan fight out their differences as they may, but don't let them in their conflict tear the Chinese Empire to pieces.[34]

Such a position was a reasonable one to take, especially since American business sold to both sides and made a profit no matter which combatant won.

The most serious aspect of the Russo-Japanese War was the chance the conflict might spread. Since the existence of both the Anglo-Japanese and Franco-Russian alliances, a European conflict was possible. *Financial Age* warned that the outbreak of a general European conflict would cause a great financial panic. "It is to be hoped that the diplomats who are guiding the destinies of Europe will keep constantly in mind the conditions with which they would be confronted in the event of an extension of the war."[35] *The Banker's Magazine,* reviewing the war at its close, also suggested that the security of the commercial and financial world had been threatened by the thought that the hostilities might spread: ". . . business enterprise has never been entirely free from apprehension of the panic and disaster that would have followed if this possible world wide war had become an actuality."[36] Because of this fear of a general European war with its resulting disruption of commerce, business was highly critical of Russia for firing on British fishing vessels at Hull. For creating this situation, one financial journal charged the Russians were acting as international criminals.[37]

During the final part of the war, business opinion differed on the question of how far the Russian situation should be allowed to deteriorate. The extreme pro-Japanese segment of business, as exemplified by the American-Asiatic Association, expressed satisfaction at the overwhelming Japanese victory. They maintained that the victory was a triumph for civilization and progress.[38] This Japanophile faction applauded every Japanese victory, as a means of bringing peace closer by showing Russia the folly of a continuing fight. Although the *Commercial and Financial Chronicle* wanted an early peace, it was opposed to a cessation of hostility unless peace gave Japan complete security against future Russian encroachments in Asia.[39]

A more moderate segment of business feared the consequences of further Japanese victories. It took the position that Russia must bring the war to an end. The *Wall Street Journal* reported that business was hostile to a continuation of the war. Consequently, the New York money market refused to lend any more to the Czar, hoping to force Russia to agree to peace terms. Although these capitalists were unwilling to support Russia further in the war, they expressed a willingness to lend money to Russia to pay for an indemnity.[40]

Russia and Japan, yielding to world pressure and to mutual exhaustion, submitted their conflict to the arbitration of President Roosevelt. The result of their decision was the long negotiations at Portsmouth, New Hampshire. The talks, which on a number of occasions threatened to break down, centered upon the Japanese demands for an indemnity and upon Japanese demands for Sakhalin Island. Business watched the negotiations, fearful that the war would break out again. For the first time since the war had begun, there were major business criticisms of the Japanese position. Most of these criticisms were directed at the Japanese demand for an indemnity. *Financial Age,* for example, observed:

> it is apparent that for purely business reasons American financial and commercial interests are not anxious for Russia to accept the peace terms laid down by her victorious enemy. Japan's demands point, in the opinion of many business men, to a complete Japanese control, commercially as well as politically, of Manchuria and

18

Korea, if not, indeed of China itself and all its dependencies. In other words, while the "open door" may exist in name . . . the United States and European nations will find themselves at a considerable disadvantage so far as their heretofore great Eastern trade is concerned.

In view of this, it is not easy to comprehend why the financial markets of the world, which take no count of lives, except in their relation to dollars, should show such evident anxiety lest Russia reject the terms which Japan has proposed. . . . But a peace such as Japan proposes might also be expensive, not only to Russia but likewise to the United States and all the nations of Europe.[41]

This editorial in *Financial Age* disagreed with the prevalent attitude during the war that Japan was defending the Open Door for America. Furthermore, *The Banker's Magazine* drew attention to the fact that Japan had waged "this desperate conflict, not for other countries, but for the protection of her own territory and the extension of her commerce and industry."[42] Both *Financial Age* and *The Banker's Magazine* indicated a suspicion of Japan as the new dominant power in the Far East. Although this suspicion was not yet prevalent throughout American business, Japan was never to enjoy the position she had held in these circles prior to the Russo-Japanese War. How far this distrust of Japan had developed among non-business observers is difficult to determine. President Roosevelt, by the end of 1905, had indicated his fear of a Japanese-dominated Orient. On the other hand, Winston Thorson in the *American Historical Review* found that most newspaper editorials after the Treaty of Portsmouth were still sympathetic to Japan.[43]

Accordingly, most commercial opinion retained an optimisitic approach toward the future of the Orient. Business was impressed by Japanese willingness to compromise with Russia, by giving up its demands for an indemnity and by accepting only half of Sakhalin, instead of holding out for the whole island. To business, the Japanese magnanimity at Portsmouth foreshadowed the opening of the Orient to the trade of all nations. The *American Exporter* expressed confidence that Japan was committed to the Open Door. Before, during, and after the war, her statesmen announced that policy, and there was no reason to doubt their sincerity.[44] Another representative of the same point of view said that American business had gained a great deal by the end of the war. Since the United States had brought the conflict to a close, it had gained the friendship of both sides; thus American business would gain through trade with both Japan and Russia.

19

But the greatest United States gain would come from a revived trade with the Orient, which was open to the commerce of the world.[45]

Meanwhile, the severest reaction against the Portsmouth Treaty came, not in Russia, but in Japan. Mobs in Tokyo, upon hearing that the treaty had been signed without the hoped-for indemnity, rioted against the government. They turned their wrath against America, which they held responsible for the final agreement. Consequently, a guard had to be placed around the American legation, and protection had to be provided for Edward Harriman, the railroad magnate, who was visiting Japan at the time the Portsmouth Treaty was signed. A few business publications sympathized with the Japanese people in their disappointment. *Asia* expressed the opinion that the Japanese were rightly disappointed at the price they had paid for peace. Never in history had a finer example of national greatness been exhibited when, for the sake of peace, Japan had humbled herself before a vanquished adversary.[46]

Although the Russo-Japanese War had proved to be costly, it appeared to some business advocates as the opening of a new era. Whether America would be able to increase its trade and consequently dispose of its surpluses due to overproduction depended on the new role of Japan. Since business viewed the Orient entirely from the standpoint of markets, the business attitude towards Japan was determined by how much commercial freedom America would have in that part of the world. To business, commercial freedom in the Orient meant the maintenance of the Open Door. The next few years would prove decisive in determining what the attitude of business would be, and consequently, would determine what the position of America would be in that region of the world.

3 FAR EASTERN PROBLEMS

The tranquility expected following the Russo-Japanese war never materialized. From 1905 to 1909, when business was hoping to capitalize on Oriental markets, a series of disturbances growing out of American restriction of Oriental immigration prevented the calm requisite for trade. The problem of American discrimination against Asians stemmed from the importation, following the Civil War, of Chinese laborers by the builders of the western railroads. When this construction had been completed, those workers settled in California, competing there for jobs with the native industrial and agricultural workers. Those persons affected, claiming that the newcomers lowered the general standard of living, lobbied through labor unions and farm organizations for restrictions against further Oriental immigration. In response to this pressure, Congress in 1882 passed the Chinese Exclusion Act, which prohibited the entry into the United States of Chinese laborers. All other Chinese nationalists, such as students and businessmen, desiring to visit the United States had to receive the approval of the American Consul in China. This approval to visit the United States was subject to reversal when the Chinese visitor reached the United States. One example of what happened under this law occurred when a group of eighty-eight Chinese merchants on their way to San Francisco were subjected to a long interrogation by immigration officials and then refused entry.[1] The Chinese merchants' reaction to such treatment was to avoid further insult by boycotting products from the United States.

Even before the boycott, business had viewed the Chinese Exclusion Act with disfavor. In 1879, the New York Chamber of Commerce had protested against the first act of Congress restricting Chinese immigration — this act was vetoed by President Rutherford B. Hayes.[2] In 1902, representatives of business petitioned Congress to change the Chinese Exclusion Act before American trade was seriously disturbed. They proposed that Chinese students and businessmen be allowed to travel in the United States without serious restrictions.[3] From 1905 to 1907, when American trade with China declined by seven million dollars because of the boycott, business took a militant stand against the restrictions. In April 1907, John Foord, secretary of the American-Asiatic Association, led a group of businessmen to Washington to appear before a Congressional committee. The delegation expressed the view that unless the United States accepted Chinese students and merchants and treated them as gentlemen, America would lose the greatest market in the world. They called for immediate action upon the part of Congress.[4]

Although most businessmen opposed the American discrimination against Chinese merchants, they were not against the basic premise which underlay the Chinese Exclusion Act. D. A. Tompkins, one of the leaders of the National Association of Manufacturers, expressed the opinion that Chinese coolie labor should be excluded. He discounted the Chinese claim that the act discriminated against the Chinese people by stating that all the United States did was to recognize in its immigration laws the same division into two classes which existed in China. Since the lower class was undesirable, the United States had a right to keep it out.[5] The National Board of Trade passed a resolution which called upon Congress to change the law so that business and professional Chinese might be admitted, but urged also that the restrictions on all Chinese laborers, skilled or unskilled, be retained.[6]

A small number of businessmen, believing the United States needed an adequate supply of cheap labor, opposed the Chinese Exclusion Act in its entirety.[7] For example, one speaker at the National Board of Trade Convention said:

> We ought to invite the Chinese here and educate their children and do all we can to get them here. The whole exclusion idea

is the idea of a very few people belonging to labor unions. It is time for the people of the United States to take into consideration and secure such legislation as will give the greatest aid in prosecuting our industries by these Chinese laborers, who are undoubtedly the best and cheapest laborers on the face of the earth.[8]

The moderate ideas of the majority of businessmen were incorporated into the Foster Amendment to the Chinese Exclusion Act. Drawn up by the American-Asiatic Association, this bill provided that businessmen and students would be issued visas at their points of departure which would be honored without question at the port of entry.[9] Although the Foster Amendment continued the exclusion of Chinese laborers from the United States, the bill was opposed by labor. When the amendment was defeated, business attacked labor for trying to destroy a very important American trade in order to prevent a few Chinese laborers from getting into the United States.[10]

While business agitated for a change in the Chinese Exclusion Act, American-Japanese relations had deteriorated. Connections between the two countries had been particularly cordial during the Russo-Japanese War, when America had contributed financially to the Japanese victory. The friendship between the countries was marred immediately after the war by the Japanese belief that the United States had prevented Japan from receiving an indemnity from Russia. The close ties between the United States and Japan disintegrated further as a result of the anti-Japanese agitation on the West Coast. When earthquake and fire destroyed San Francisco, the Board of Education took the opportunity to place the children of that city's considerable Japanese population into segregated schools. Prior to the disaster, there had been considerable opposition to the Japanese, for the same reason that resentment had developed against the Chinese. When the Japanese government protested the action of the Board of Education as violating a treaty with the United States, President Roosevelt tried to persuade San Francisco to take a more reasonable position. As a result of his failure, the comments of the "yellow press" made it appear that war was imminent.

Business was more disturbed by this clash with Tokyo than it had been by the Chinese boycott of American goods. Since Japan was one of America's best customers, any break with it would be the loss of an actual market, not just a hoped for one, as with China. Thus business condemned the action of San Francisco as being a most unjust and unreasonable one. It has done incalculable harm in arousing the enmity of a people with whom we have been on the terms of the closest international friendship for more than half a century . . . harm must result to American business' interests. It will prove especially damaging to the agricultural and manufacturing interests of the cotton growing States (*sic.*), for it will practically shut the door to Korea, Manchuria, China and Japan for our cotton products, our grain and our agricultural implements. The United States cannot afford to make enemies in support of an unjust cause.[11]

The Boston Chamber of Commerce supported this statement, hoping that every effort would be made to promote the commercial relations between the two countries.[12] Meanwhile, the National Board of Trade, sympathizing with the President's inability to compel San Francisco to accept a reasonable settlement, petitioned Congress to give the Executive Branch more power to enable it to carry out treaty obligations which are impaired by local actions.[13]

Besides using its influence against San Francisco, business tried to prevent the issue of Japanese segregation from becoming the basis for a conflict between the United States and Japan. The commercial press tried to minimize the war rumors circulated by the "yellow journalists." Accordingly the *American Exporter* called the incident a "tempest in a teapot," which had no international significance but was purely a local affair.[14] The *Commercial and Financial Chronicle* accused "yellow journalism" newspapers of creating a misunderstanding between the United States and Japan, just to see a conflict occur.[15]

Just as business disliked any action that would disturb the peace between the United States and Japan, so it opposed President Roosevelt's sending a fleet to Japan. *The Banker's Magazine* discounted Roosevelt's announcement that the voyage was a training mission. The most important objective of the United States, advised this periodical, was to keep the two peoples in an amicable frame of mind, not to be achieved by displaying American naval forces. If war did not develop from Roosevelt's ill-advised action, Japan would still have cause to distrust and dislike the United States.[16] The *Commercial and Financial Chronicle* similarly condemned President Roosevelt, but hoped that the visit of Secretary of War William Howard Taft to Japan would restore cordial relations between the two countries.[17]

Although Roosevelt's conclusion of the "Gentlemen's Agreement" temporarily ended the agitation over Japanese immigra-

24

tion and Japanese segregation, a new disturbance which threatened the peace occurred in California. A series of laws restricting Japanese from being property owners or businessmen in California was introduced into the state legislature. Consequently, the National Board of Trade announced its opposition to

> any and all legislation intended to discriminate against Japan or her citizens, but on the contrary it is believed that every effort should be made to cultivate and promote the most intimate commercial relations between the two countries and that all the privileges now enjoyed by the most favored nation should continue to be extended to the Japanese.[18]

The New York Chamber of Commerce condemned the action of California as dishonorable because it violated the terms of an international treaty.[19]

The anti-Japanese bills failed to pass the California legislature because of the pressure brought against them by business interests in the state. The San Francisco Real Estate Board, the San Francisco Merchants Association, and most California chambers of commerce and boards of trade were against the laws.[20] The Merchants Association of San Francisco represented the majority of California businessmen in a letter to the state legislature which said:

> California, and, in fact, the entire Pacific Coast by reason of its geographical position, must look to the development of trade with the Orient as its greatest commercial asset of the future, and any measure would be unwise which is calculated to antagonize unnecessarily the very people with whom it is to our interests to develop trade relations.[21]

California commercial interests had come to realize that the West Coast would be harmed the most by a decline in America's Oriental trade. Thus California business groups were able to force the state legislature to follow a moderate policy toward the Japanese.

Even more serious than California's anti-Japanese legislation in disturbing the cordial relations between the United States and Japan was the clash of interests between the two nations in Asia. Japan, as a result of the Russo-Japanese War, had been left in control of large areas of Manchuria and all of Korea. In 1905, after the conclusion of the Treaty of Portsmouth, there was a general belief that in these regions Japan would live up to the principles of the Open Door. In fact, business throughout the Russo-Japanese War was convinced that Japan was defending the Open Door for the rest of civilization. John Hays Hammond, a mining expert and financier, expressed skepticism at what he considered the naiveté of business. He warned, "The strategic position which Japan will have obtained commercially by reason of the suzerainty, if not, indeed, the ownership, she will have established in Korea, and possibly Manchuria also, will render her our most formidable competitor in the Far East,"[22]

The first evidence of the truth of Hammond's statement came in Korea. American investors there had been assured by the Japanese government that legitimate foreign investments would be treated fairly and on an equal level with those of native firms. Contrary to her promise, however, Japan initiated a policy of repression and discrimination in an attempt to drive out foreign concerns. One American firm to be mistreated by the Japanese was Colburn and Bostick, which operated the Seoul street railroad system and had other utility and mining concessions. When Colburn and Bostick refused to sell out its interests at a price named by Japan, the government began a policy of hindrance and obstruction against the company. The American business was prevented from taking claim to a mining concession it had received from the previous government; a competing telephone company was established, and the Japanese began a campaign to discredit the American firm.[23] Other American companies in Korea met with similar difficulties. For example, rebates were given to Japanese firms in Korea from the governmentally operated railroad. Furthermore, the Japanese government allowed their firms to imitate American trade-marks.[24]

Manchuria was even more important to American business than Korea. Consequently, a year after the end of the Russo-Japanese War, a committee of American merchants visited Manchuria and reported to Washington that Japan was discriminating against American goods. This committee found a situation similar to that in Korea, in which Japanese business groups were given railroad rebates and lowered import duty rates.[25] The American-Asiatic Association verified this account, adding that Japanese goods had been carried free, or at reduced rates, on the Chinese Eastern railroad and that a free port in Manchuria had been opened to Japanese goods. These actions not only put American goods at a disadvantage, but threatened the whole Chinese customs system.[26] American goods were put at a further disadvantage by the circulation of Japanese war notes in Manchuria, thus inducing the purchase of Japanese goods, and the copying of American trade-marks by Japanese merchants.

While many business leaders viewed the Japanese behavior with concern, the majority of them remained in favor of continued cordial Japanese-American relations. However, a vocal business minority became anti-Japanese. The *American Exporter,* for example, represented this minority in expressing the belief that the next great war would come in the Pacific with the United States as an active or moral supporter of the nation in the right.

> Japanese intentions seem aimed at China. We may perhaps swallow with the traditional and appropriate pinch of salt the smoothly inane platitudes of our own and Japanese diplomats rehearsing over and over again the familiar text of 'traditional friendship,' but the fact will remain that the United States is and must continue to be a stumbling block in the way of Japanese progress in the direction she seems bent on pursuing roughshod over the integrity of the Celestial Empire.[27]

This opinion represented a sharp change from the *American Exporter*'s earlier stand in 1905, when it maintained that Japanese supervision in Manchuria and Korea would open a new field of trade for the United States. Its later position resembles the business attitude towards Russia five years before. To the segment of business represented by the *American Exporter,* Japan had replaced Russia as the great threat to Chinese integrity and to the Open Door.[28]

The American-Asiatic Association, which represented those businessmen who hoped for continued friendly relations between the United States and Japan, denied that the Japanese in Manchuria could be compared to the Russians there prior to the Russo-Japanese War. All Japan was interested in was peaceful trade whereas Russia had been trying to seize Manchurian territory.[29] The *Journal of Commerce* also maintained that the two situations were dissimilar. Nothing had happened in the Orient to warrant the attitude that Japan was not living up to the principles of the Open Door. However, this periodical did want the American government to observe the situation and protest if Japan should discriminate against American goods.[30] Even the American-Asiatic Association was ready to follow this advice. When Japan refused to allow China to build the Fakumen to Hsinmintun Railroad on the grounds that is interfered with the rights of the Southern Manchurian Railroad, *Asia* warned Japan that the opinion of the world was against her.

It also expressed the hope that this policy was not aimed to check China's national progress.[31]

As with the earlier problems of immigration and segregation of the Japanese, the major fear of business was that hostilities would break out between the two nations. Business was concerned especially about the books and magazine articles after 1905 which emphasized as inevitable conflict between the United States and Japan. Business was eager to demonstrate the existence of cordial relations between the two countries. The *Journal of Commerce* used the Root-Takahira Agreement as an example of the complete accord on eastern Asia between Japan and the United States. This periodical pointed to the common desire of both nations to disclaim aggressive designs on the territory of the other or on an outside power. There "never had been any divergence between this Government and that of Japan in regard to the broad lines of policy to be followed in Eastern Asia."[32] The *New York Commercial* also greeted the agreement as a demonstration of the friendship of the two nations, and it expressed also the hope that the concord would quiet the jingoists of both nations. [33]

A committee was appointed by the chambers of commerce of the Pacific Coast to go to Japan to obtain a first-hand account of conditions in the Island Empire. This committee brought back information which did much to eliminate talk of a conflict between the United States and Japan. The group reported that any conflict between the two countries would be impossible. During its stay, the committee was impressed by the signs of friendship expressed toward the United States. The friendship the committee reported was based on the gratitude owed to the United States by the Japanese people resulting from American help to Japan during the Russo-Japanese War.[34] To further the cause of peace between the two countries, many prominent businessmen joined in forming the Japan Society in New York City. Under the editorship of Lord Lindsay Russell, the Japan Society published a collection of articles by prominent men, especially in the field of business, glorifying the ties of friendship between Japan and the United States.[35]

Before and after the Russo-Japanese War, American business had indicated its desire that Chinese integrity be maintained, so that this market would be kept open to American trade. Accordingly businessmen had tried to influence the government to act in their behalf. Otherwise, they warned, the overproduction of American industries would have no outlets. The government at this time did act on a number of occasions to protect American business interests in the Orient. But all this would have been to no avail if business had been unwilling to act in its own behalf. Business leaders, from the end of the Spanish-American War to the outbreak of World War I, engaged in various schemes, all aimed at establishing American equality on the Asian continent. These activities indicate the attitude of an important segment of the business community and of the methods they hoped would keep American opportunities open in Asia.

America's first commitment in China was through the American China Development Company. Organized in 1895 by James Stillman of the National City Bank, Charles Coster of J. P. Morgan and Company, Edward Harriman, and Jacob Schiff, this firm received a concession from the Chinese government permitting them to build a railroad from Hankow to Canton. Although the American China Development Company made elaborate surveys of the proposed line, it built few tracks. American investors were still unprepared to undertake foreign financial adventures, and little capital was recruited to finance this project. Not only was little money raised to build the railroad, but American investors lost control of the company when a Belgian banking firm gained control of a majority of the shares of the enterprise. As a consequence of this change in ownership, the Chinese government threatened to cancel the charter of the company. Reasoning that this action would be detrimental to American interests in the Orient, President Roosevelt pressured J. P. Morgan and Company to regain control of the American China Development Company. Despite this plea, Morgan, after buying back control of the firm, negotiated an agreement with China for the Company's liquidation.[36] Considering the concern business had shown about an American penetration of the Orient, there was little interest in this project, an enterprise which could have gone far towards achieving that goal. Only the New York *Journal of Commerce and Commercial Bulletin* expressed disappointment that the Chinese-American Development Company had failed to win the support of business.[37]

Edward Harriman was not deterred by the failure of this project. His interest in the Orient stemmed from his control of the Union Pacific and Southern Pacific railroads. Both Harriman and his chief rival on the Pacific Coast, James J. Hill, wanted an increase in America's Far Eastern trade. Such an increase

29

would bring profits to both railroad systems. Since Harriman controlled a group of trans-Pacific steamship lines, he had an additional interest in the Far East.

By using his steamship and his railroads as a base, Harriman hoped to create a transportation network that would go around the world. Harriman planned to complete this transportation chain by acquiring facilities in Manchuria, Siberia, European Russia, Europe, and the Atlantic Ocean. When this system was completed, America would be able to take a commanding position in the Orient and would be able to supply the needs of millions of people living in the underdeveloped areas.[38] It might appear that Harriman's plans were a fantastic fabrication of the mind, but in an era which saw the creation of numerous trusts an extension of American high finance to the rest of the world seemed only logical. Futhermore, since trade follows transportation routes, Harriman's projected system would do much to end any threat of overproduction and assure a market for American industry.

Harriman's attention was again focused on the Orient in 1905 by the American Minister to Tokyo, Lloyd C. Griscom. Griscom sent Harriman a cable warning him that the Japanese expansion would mean an end to American commercial interests in the Pacific unless something was done to prevent this from happening.[39] Griscom's plea to take some action in the Far East initiated a period of close collaboration between American diplomats and businessmen. Both groups had come to the realization that the American pronouncement of an "open door" was not enough to reserve China for American commerce. China could be saved only by a more vigorous penetration of the Orient by American enterprise. Consequently, Harriman decided to go to Japan to investigate the Far Eastern situation and to negotiate the purchase of the Southern Manchurian Railroad, which Japan had acquired from Russia as part of the Treaty of Portsmouth. He wanted to use the railroad as a link in his global rail system by connecting it to the Russian controlled Chinese Eastern Railroad and to the Trans-Siberian, where he hoped to obtain trackage rights. The most difficult part of this project was to persuade Japan to sell the Southern Manchurian Railroad. Since the line was in poor condition and Japan had little money to repair it, Harriman thought that Japan would agree to the sale.[40]

Harriman reached a preliminary agreement with the Japanese Prime Minister, which gave an American syndicate equal rights with the Japanese government to the railroad and to the development of industry and mines along its tracks.[41] By signing the agreement, it appeared that Japan had recognized the United States as being on a par with her in Manchuria. Furthermore, Harriman believed that his control over Russia's Chinese Eastern Railroad would prevent Russia or Japan from destroying Chinese control over Manchuria. Unfortunately for Harriman, the Japanese Foreign Minister, Komura, who had just returned from Portsmouth, disavowed the agreement as inconsistent with the Russo-Japanese Treaty.[42] Actually, the official explanation for Komura's breaking of the contract with Harriman hid the real reason for this action, the dissatisfaction of the Japanese people with the Treaty of Portsmouth. Although this defeat temporarily cooled Harriman's ardor for a global railroad, his project was not forgotten. Instead he turned to other capitalists and to the United States government to help him in accomplishing his penetration of Manchuria.

The next attempt of business to penetrate China was aided by the American government. One high official of the State Department called this close cooperation between government and business necessary to the continued growth of the United States. Because America's need for foreign trade was increasing, foreign markets were becoming more and more important to its manufacturers.[43] As a consequence of a decade of propagandizing by business, representatives of the American government had accepted the theory of overproduction and were willing to take the lead in keeping open markets for American manufacturers. Willard Straight, the American Consul in Manchuria, became the symbol of the close cooperation between American diplomats and American business. He felt that American capital was required in Manchuria in order to offset the influence of the Japanese.[44] To this end, Straight became an enthusiastic supporter of Harriman's attempt to gain control of the two Manchurian railroads. The Consul formulated a plan to aid the railroad magnate. Acting independently, Straight suggested to the Chinese Foreign Minister Tang Shao-yi that a Manchurian Bank be created with a capitalization of 20 million dollars, financed by a loan from American bankers. Straight's plan also called for the construction of a railroad from Hsinmintun to Changchung and then to the Trans-Siberian Railroad, thus running parallel to the Japanese controlled Southern Manchurian Railroad. This project if completed would give China independence from Japan, provide for the introduction of American capital, and give Harriman his connection to the Trans-Siberian Railroad.[45]

Straight urged Harriman to aid Tang in securing the money to set up the bank, but the Panic of 1907 prevented the railroad king from rendering assistance. Meanwhile, Tang, hoping to rid China of Japanese domination, was persuaded by Straight to visit the United States. Although he found the American government less cooperative than Straight had been, Tang received a cordial welcome from American business. Since the 1907 slump had ended, Wall Street again looked to foreign lands in which to invest surplus capital. Therefore, after being the guest of honor at an American-Asiatic Association banquet, Tang was approached by Schiff and Harriman, who were interested in the loan. However, before an agreement could be reached, Tang was recalled by his government.[46]

Following Tang's return to China, Jacob Schiff became interested in a plan to have the Chinese government purchase the Chinese Eastern Railroad. Schiff believed that this Chinese purchase would solidify the Root-Takahira agreement between the United States and Japan by eliminating one source of friction between them. Under Schiff's idea, America would become the stockholder of the main lines of communication between northern and southern Manchuria. Schiff felt that all parties would gain by this arrangement. Russia was losing money on the railroad and wished to rid herself of it. For Japan, Schiff held out the benefit of a considerable debt reduction if the Southern Manchurian Railroad were bought with American capital.[47] In reply to his inquiry to Japan about a sale of the Southern Manchurian Railroad, Schiff received a brisk communique from Baron Shibusane, advising him to abandon all further activity because Japan could not consider selling the railroad since it was necessary to its security.[48] Schiff's failure to achieve an American stewardship over the Manchurian railroads put an end to the individual efforts of Harriman and Schiff to achieve railroad supremacy in Manchuria.

When representatives of German, British, and French financial groups announced that they had arranged the financing of a Hankow to Canton railroad, American financiers protested to the State Department. The basis of their protestation was that they had previously received a promise from the Chinese government that they would be allowed to finance the first part of a railroad from Hankow to Szechuen. This protest was forwarded to the Chinese government. Consequently, when the European banking combination and Peking seemed amenable to American participation in the venture, Washington called upon J. P. Morgan and Company, the National City Bank, Kuhn, Loeb and Company, the First National Bank, and Edward H. Harriman to participate as the American group in the financing of the railroad. All of these firms had already taken part in Chinese financial affairs when asked by the State Department. Consequently, there was some criticism of the State Department's action by businessmen left outside the American group. Representatives of the International Banking Corporation, which had been interested in China for many years, condemned the American government for penetrating areas in which it had no right to enter. Washington was also criticized for being the commercial representative of J. P. Morgan and Company.[49]

Before the American group signed an agreement with the other banking combinations, there was some disagreement as to how great American participation should be. For the purpose of compromise, the United States firms were willing to take a lesser share than the other countries, but the State Department intervened, refusing to allow the American group to join on any grounds except on equal terms with the other three combinations. Washington believed that anything less than equality in the whole project would hinder American claims to equality in future Chinese projects. By this action, the American government indicated that it was more interested in protecting the rights of business than those of the firms involved. Because of the American pressure, the other financial combinations agreed to an equal share for the Americans of a six million pound loan.[50]

The American-Asiatic Association viewed the entrance of the American group into the building of the Chinese railroad as an important part of the plan to maintain the integrity of China.

> It is . . . very much in the interests of China itself that a power so deeply concerned in maintaining the integrity of the Empire, and so absolutely destitute of any desire for territorial aggrandizement at its expense, as the United States should be a party to negotiations which may have an important bearing on the future control of Chinese finance.[51]

Differing with the American-Asiatic Association, the *American Exporter* questioned whether American participation in the loan would contribute to an increased American trade with China. "The entry of American financial institutions into foreign fields in any other way than through the establishment of the usual commercial banks will not, then, arouse any extraordinary enthusiasm in the country, unless it is made clear that something more than a speculation in bonds is involved."[52]

33

Meanwhile, Secretary of State Knox, taking his ideas from the schemes of Harriman, Schiff, and Straight for a Chinese-American control over the Manchurian railroads, proposed that an international syndicate lend money for the purchase of all Manchurian railroads on China's behalf. Knox's neutralization proposal met the same fate as Harriman's earlier plans. The main force working against the Secretary of State was the final consolidation of the Triple Entente before World War I. Consequently both Japan and Russia rejected Knox's railroad proposal on the same day and in the same language. Furthermore, the rejection of Knox's suggestions was followed up by the Russo-Japanese Pact which promised mutual consultation in protection of the *status quo* and cooperation in Manchurian railroad development.[53]

Business reacted unfavorably to the alliance between the two former enemies. Jacob Schiff censured Japan for its ingratitude to the Americans who had financed the war against Russia.[54] Even the American-Asiatic Association protested that it was ironic that the equilibrium of the world had to be purchased at the expense of China by Japan, which had only recently waged a war to defend the integrity of China, "and with the tacit approval of another power [England] whose commercial interests, like our own, had steadily demanded the maintenance of the Open Door throughout the whole Chinese Empire."[55]

After Knox's scheme to neutralize the railroads of Manchuria failed, the American group was invited by the French, British, and German banking combinations to join in the formation of the International Banking Consortium in October, 1910. The new financial bloc agreed to create a 50 million dollar fund to be used in reforming Chinese currency and in initiating an industrial development plan for Manchuria. Davison of the American group informed Secretary of State Knox that United States participation in the Consortium would produce important results for American business interests. Schiff also felt that the loan would go a long way towards advancing America's prestige in the Far East. He stated that this objective was far more important to the bankers than making a profit in the venture.[56]

The difficulties which beset the International Banking Consortium made success in their venture to stabilize the Chinese economy impossible.[57] Because of opposition by Chinese nationalist groups to foreign influence, a revolt broke out against the central government. This instability made the Peking authorities more difficult to deal with than before. Although one part of the contract with China gave the Consortium a monopoly of all Chinese borrowing, the Chinese government made a number of concessions to non-Consortium firms for loans. Furthermore, quarrels among the members of the various participants of the international banking alliance added to its difficulties. The Consortium was further disturbed by the pressure brought upon it by Russia and Japan who were anxious to gain a part of the loans. A final difficulty was the inability of the Consortium to dispose of the Chinese bonds.

The American group experienced much hardship itself and threatened to withdraw from the banking combination on a number of occasions. Only the intervention of Secretary Knox prevented this from happening. With the election of Woodrow Wilson as President, the period of "dollar diplomacy" came to an end. Consequently William Jennings Bryan, the new Secretary of State, informed the American group that their activities were detrimental to Chinese political independence and to American policy. With the loss of governmental backing, the American group withdrew completely from the field of Chinese finance. This failure of American capital to make any formidable penetration in China, coinciding as it did with the outbreak of World War I, ended temporarily American business interest in China.

Although the business interests of the United States were not successful in their plans to maintain China as a market for their goods by investing capital there, they did win the support of the government for their program. As a consequence, the government was able to use its influence to keep the Chinese Empire open to American trade. Although China remained available for American commerce, the collaboration between business and government was not able to achieve any lasting penetration. By 1913, the full possibility of China as a market for American goods had not been realized. Although exports to the area had doubled since 1901, they remained only a small part of the total American trade.[58] Nevertheless, the commercial foreign policy formulated in the period prior to World War I was the foundation upon which American relations in the Far East was based following that conflict. As a result of the interest of American business in the markets of the Far East, it also became concerned with other potential markets, particularly in Latin America.

4 BUSINESS LOOKS AT LATIN AMERICA

Business interest in Latin America as well as in the Orient was motivated by the same fear of overproduction. To increase foreign trade, which was absorbing only five per cent of America's total production, John Hays Hammond recommended that the United States follow the path of least resistance and endeavor to increase its commerce with Latin America. Hammond urged a revived Western Hemisphere trade as an alternative to the American practice of dumping surplus goods below price in the home markets of European business rivals. An active trade with Central and South America would also be insurance for the future, when retaliatory tariffs would curtail American trade with Europe.[1] To John Barrett, director of the International Bureau of American Republics, Latin America was more than just insurance against the loss of the European market. He saw in the Hispanic republics seventy-five million customers who were ready and able to purchase the United States' industrial products. In return for these, Latin America could give the United States many raw materials.

Barrett illustrated the great potential of Latin American trade in contrast to that of Asia with the case of Argentina. Although it had a population of only sixteen million people, Argentina had a greater foreign commerce than either Japan or China.[2]

The failure of American business to compete successfully with England and Germany was discussed frequently in commercial periodicals and at trade conventions. *Iron Age* warned American industrialists not to lose sight of Latin America as a market for goods manufactured in the United States. This periodical expressed regret that so much emphasis had been placed on action by the government as a means of securing this lucrative market. Although steamship subsidies and reciprocity acts were needed, the best way of obtaining Latin American trade was to acquaint the people there with American products.[3]

In trading with Latin America, manufacturers were urged to produce especially for this market and not to send them surplus products. Goods which were well packed to withstand the long

36

journey from factory to market were also considered a necessity. Manufacturers were told to send salesmen to Latin America who could speak their language.[4]

As a further step in facilitating the growth of an export trade with Latin America, it was suggested at numerous trade conventions that the United States follow the lead of Great Britain and invest in commercial enterprises south of the Rio Grande. By investing enormous sums in Argentinean and Brazilian businesses, Britain had trebled the volume of her trade in those areas, thus proving that "trade follows the investment of a nation's capital as well as a nation's flag."[5]

The proponents of business expansion thought that the establishment of branches of United States banks in Latin America was necessary to the development of trade with these countries. Prior to the passage of the Federal Reserve Act, national banks had no authority to establish overseas branches. Although some of the states granted this right to banks chartered under their jurisdiction, all of the larger American financial institutions were national banks. Consequently, *The Banker's Magazine* suggested,

> In view of the awakening of American interest in foreign commerce and enterprise, especially in the direction of the Latin American countries, it would seem that the time has come when our banking system might be made more elastic so as to permit its extension to other countries where our trade interests are destined soon to witness an enormous expansion.[6]

The need for overseas bank branches was great because foreign financial institutions in Latin America acted as commercial agents in expanding the trade of their countries.[7] After the passage of the Federal Reserve Act, branches of United States' banks were organized throughout Latin America.

In contrast to the small increase in trade to China, American exports expanded steadily to the nations south of the Rio Grande. The value of these exports to South America increased from forty-four million dollars in 1902 to one hundred and forty-six million dollars in 1913. There was a comparable increase in exports to the Caribbean countries, to Mexico and to Central America.[8] The belief of Hammond and Barrett that Latin America would become the most important market of the United States seemed to have been justified. The reason for the contrast with China lies in the ability of Latin America to pay for their imports from the United States with exports of their own.

Along with the increase in exports to Latin America, there

was a corresponding rise in American investments there. By 1913, the value of American investments in Mexico alone increased in value from one hundred and eighty-five million dollars to over one billion dollars.[9]

These large investments came to play an increasingly important part in the conduct of American foreign affairs and in the attitude that business held toward Latin America. Moreover, a number of problems developed as a result of this expansion of United States business to Latin America. One such problem was the relationship the United States company should maintain with the Latin American country in which it had invested. The complexity of the situation can be seen when it is remembered that some companies had more capital at their disposal than did their host countries. This condition often led to manipulation by the companies of the internal affairs of the countries in which they had invested capital. Another problem concerned the amount of protection the United States government should provide for its nationals. In areas often beset with revolutions and generally unstable government, this was a vital factor.

The major United States investments were in the extracting industries. North American concerns were particularly active in exploiting Mexican petroleum, Venezuelan asphalt, and Bolivian tin. Relations between the concerns and the individual countries were determined by a contract whose provisions were enforced in the local courts. An example of such a contract was one granted to the Petroleum Company of Sonora by the Mexican government. The concern was granted a large area in Sonora province. It had twenty years in which to explore for petroleum. If petroleum were discovered, the company was granted the right to lay claim to 2,000 hectares surrounding the claim, even if part of the claim were on private property. In return for these privileges, the Sonora Company agreed to pay the Mexican government ten per cent of the revenue it grossed from its wells. In addition, the company was to pay an annual fee of five dollars per hectare.[10] A similar contract was signed by an American company, the United States and Venezuela Company of New Jersey and Venezuelan President Castro. The American concession included the right to explore for asphalt and to build a railroad. Furthermore, the government granted the concern a ninety-nine year lease on the asphalt mine and freedom from taxation on the railroad and from import duties on materials for building it.[11]

In addition to those investing in the extractive industries, there were other important American investments in Latin America. For example, Willian Randell received a thirty year concession to build and to operate the street railroads in Bogota, Colombia. Moreover, Americans operated electric power plants in Mariro and Coli, in Colombia.[12]

The bankers who purchased Japanese bonds set an example for their colleagues who now loaned considerable sums to Latin American governments. Because of the instability of these governments, a contract providing for a means of raising revenue in case the loans were in default was negotiated along with the terms of the loan. For example, the contract between Speyer and Company and Cuba contained a specification that Cuba put aside fifteen per cent of her customs receipts plus any other custom funds to equal $85,000 a month towards the repayment of the debt. Despite this provision, the bankers and their agents were forbidden to interfere with custom receipts.[13]

In addition to loaning money, United States banks provided other services. Brown Brothers and J. W. Seligman and Company, under the auspices of their government, arranged with Nicaragua to revise its monetary system and to put the country's financial organization on a sound basis. Two currency experts, F. C. Harrison and C. Conant were sent to Nicaragua. After surveying the situation, they submitted reports to their firms and to the President of Nicaragua. The report was adopted by the national legislature.[14]

The outstanding United States firm in Latin America was the United Fruit Company. This concern, the result of a consolidation of a number of small firms in the 1890's, monopolized by 1904 ninety per cent of the banana trade. In Costa Rica alone, the United Fruit Company employed over seven thousand natives on fifty thousand acres, which yielded eleven million stems.[15] As a consequence of its vast holdings, the United Fruit Company was able to exert a powerful influence over the countries in which it operated. One example of the United Fruit Company's strength was demonstrated in its struggle with the American Banana Company. This concern attempted to challenge the supremacy of the United Fruit Company with a grant in banana lands it received from the Panamanian government. Consequently, Costa Rica laid claim to these lands and attempted to drive the American Banana Company from them. The American Banana Company questioned the claim of Costa Rica and charged that it had acted under the influence of the United Fruit Company.

39

Before the dispute was finally settled, Costa Rica and Panama had submitted their case to the Hague; the United States State Department had sent a note of warning to Costa Rica, and the Supreme Court and Senate of the United States had reviewed the case. In examining the dispute, Kepner concluded, "One of the unfortunate results of foreign investments in Central America has been the intensification of boundary disputes."[16] Thus, a conflict between American companies became an international controversy, since both Panama and Costa Rica had entered into this dispute on behalf of the two American enterprises. The attitude of the American Banana Company in this case is interesting. The company, in its competition with the United Fruit Company, attempted to use the power of the United States government. It called upon the State Department and the American courts to gain for it the justice it alleged it was not getting from Costa Rica.[17]

Most United States businessmen regarded a promise of government aid in case it was needed as a prerequisite for doing business in Latin America. Because of the unstable financial and political structure of the Latin American republics, there were a great many disputes between United States firms and the countries in which they had invested capital. Consequently, the question was raised as to what type of protection the United States should provide these firms. Mortimer Schiff, of Kuhn, Loeb and Company, presented the opinion of financiers on the subject. Schiff said it had been a great comfort to European investors to know that if a foreign government failed to live up to its obligations an individual could expect his government to "back him up diplomatically and even otherwise in enforcing his just demands. The courts are not open to international financiers . . . and our ships must unfortunately take the place of receiverships and foreclosures. Until we can feel certain that our government will maintain the rights of American citizens, who have made legitimate investments in foreign countries, it is hopeless to try to create here a rich market for foreign securities." Schiff also felt that the inaction of the government in the area of investor protection had "done more to militate against foreign investments by our public than all the talk of America as the eventual financial center of the world does to encourage them."[18] John Hays Hammond wrote, "Now, in order to stimulate the investment of capital in foreign lands it is a prerequisite that the investor be assured of protection by his government against any unfair interference or discrimination on the part of foreign governments where these investments are made."[19] These two business leaders, both of whom believed that the United States could only survive economically by expanding its trade and investments abroad, were equally convinced that unless their government supported business by protecting its overseas investments, business could not encourage this expansion.

Because business believed that foreign investment and government protection went hand in hand, there was universal commercial opposition to the Drago Doctrine and the Calvo Clause. The *Journal of Commerce and Commercial Bulletin* denied the basic premise of these two doctrines: that all sovereign states are free and equal, and that interference by one nation within another nation is not an act of justice, but an act of might. The *Journal* wrote, "while nations may be held to be free, they may not be so free as to act with injustice toward other nations or their citizens. Moreover, nations are not equal in the sense that they are equal in honesty, equal in integrity and equal in a sense of justice any more than they are equal in wealth or in numbers or in power." Until a court is created to safeguard international relations, "the admission must be made that there are fundamental reasons of justice and of public policy to sustain the right to the exercise of force to comply restitution of contract claims under international law."[20]

The most flagrant violations of the rights of United States businessmen in Latin America occurred in Venezuela during the Castro administration. Castro's disregard for international law had almost brought a European intervention to that country. Consequently, his actions against North American businessmen brought demands for action by the government of the United States. The most forceful denunciations of the Castro regime came from the New York Bermudez Company. This firm had signed a typical contract with Venezuela, granting the concern the right to exploit a field of asphalt for ninety-nine years. The company also had the right to build a railroad, on which the government enjoyed special privileges. After investing over one million dollars in Venezuela, the company began making a profit. Subsequently, President Castro, who was trying to suppress a revolution, made a number of financial demands on the company. Moreover, he ordered the courts to seize the concern's property which he turned over to a rival firm of which he was a stockholder. The New York Bermudez Company's appeal was rejected by the highest court in Venezuela.[21] The company then appealed to the United States government to in-

41

tervene in order to secure justice. The company charged that the courts, which were controlled by Castro, had acted without integrity.[22]

Castro's disregard for American property in Venezuela received a great deal of criticism in the commercial press. These periodicals urged the State Department to intervene in order to protect the rights of United States businessmen who suffered from Castro's seizure of their property and his contract violations. Yielding to these requests, the State Department protested against these seizures to Venezuela. When this failed, the companies' claims were submitted to the Hague Court of Arbitration. In commenting on the cases before the Hague Court, the *Commercial and Financial Chronicle* urged Venezuela to realize that when a nation accepts *de facto* recognition it also undertakes the responsibility for visitors and their property. If Venezuela did not fulfill its obligations, the other nations had a right to collect damages.[23] *Bradstreet's* warned Venezuela that the Hague Court would offer no resistance to the forcible collection by the United States of its debts. Venezuela and other weak nations were advised to avoid any action that might bring on foreign intervention.[24] The same periodical, a year later, advised Venezuela to give Amesican claims serious consideration.[25]

The malpractices of President Castro presented the United States government with a second problem. When he defaulted on Venezuela's debts to German, English, and Italian creditors, the question of American responsibilities under the Monroe Doctrine was raised. The *Commercial and Financial Chronicle* saw three alternative solutions to this problem: (1) Allow the creditors to use force in collecting their debts. (2) Arbitration by the Hague Court. (3) Arbitration by the United States. This periodical noted that there was a great danger to the United States in alternatives one and three. Forcible collection of the debts by the European powers would be a violation of the Monroe Doctrine. If the United States arbitrated the dispute and found in favor of Venezuela, there would be difficulties with Europe. If the Europeans won, the United States would have to collect the debt themselves.[26]

The *American Banker* agreed that the United States should not intervene in Venezuela, but it felt that Venezuela had invoked the Monroe Doctrine too many times already. This periodical desired to see Germany given a free hand to collect her debts without taking any territory.[27]

The *Marine Journal*, which was impatient with the Castro

42

regime because of the damage it had done to American shipping, took a broader point of view. It concluded that the United States, in keeping with the Monroe Doctrine, should either allow the creditors to collect their own debts in Venezuela, or guarantee the debt collection.[28]

Isaac Seligman of J. and W. Seligman and Company carried the *Marine Journal's* proposal to its logical conclusion. He said, "We must logically see to it that European debts are satisfactorily settled, as otherwise our insistence on the Monroe Doctrine will subject us to embarrassing, if not serious complications." At the time of the Venezuelan crisis, few businessmen were willing to support Mr. Seligman's far-reaching conclusion.[29]

While most businessmen did not favor intervention in South America in support of the Monroe Doctrine, they were ready to support such intervention in the Caribbean area. American businessmen had important investments and trade connections in this part of the world. The Caribbean was also a vital link in the defenses of the Panama Canal, a vital factor in the development of American commerce.

Business interest in the new Roosevelt theory of the Monroe Doctrine reached a peak with the crisis in the Dominican Republic. The conditions on this island nation were similar to those in Venezuela. A series of revolutions and debt defaults had incited threats of European intervention. Moreover, rebellious forces fired at steamships of the Clyde Line, an American concern. American commerce immediately demanded the United States provide for the safety of its merchant vessels trading in this area.[30]

When, in 1904, a financial crisis in the Dominican Republic made European intervention imminent, Roosevelt declared the Roosevelt Corollary. Moreover, he signed an agreement with the Dominican Republic providing for the United States administration of the customs collection and debt payments. Commercial spokesmen supported both the Corollary and the treaty. For example, the New York Board of Trade supported the treaty because it considered the Dominican Republic incapable of solving its problems alone. Furthermore, if the United States did not aid the Dominican Republic, some other country probably would. The Board contended that the United States would do the job with the least interference into the affairs of the Republic. The Board also felt that the treaty would benefit the United States-Latin America trade, by providing a market for surplus goods. In addition, the treaty was "a step in the right direction of that influence for good which the United States may be called upon to exert upon those of our southern neighbors whose relations with the countries of Europe may constitute . . . a threat to our tranquility and commerce."[31]

Both the New York and Philadelphia boards of trade agreed with the principle of United States responsibility for the maintenance of order in the Caribbean as stated in the Roosevelt Corollary. The Philadelphia Board pointed out the removal of the threat of European intervention would also remove the danger to American trade in that island and to the south of it.[32] The *Wall Street Journal* concurred in the opinion that the United States had to assume new responsibilities in connection with the Monroe Doctrine. Without firm leadership, the United States could not make that doctrine effective as an instrument of peace. Roosevelt, in this publication's view, had shown great wisdom in shaping foreign policy.[33] The *American Exporter* answered charges that the United States was acting as a policeman in Latin America by characterizing these accusations as "unwarranted, for there is a vast difference between the officer who patrols his beat club in hand" and a disinterested citizen who climbs a fence to bring about peace.[34]

Not all business groups considered President Roosevelt to be following a farsighted policy. The *Protectionist* criticized the premise on which the Corollary was based.

> While the action of our government in the Santo Domingo case may be justified by circumstances, it is to be hoped that it will not establish a precedent for our engaging in the debt collecting business in other countries for the benefit of foreign creditors and American speculators.[35]

The *Commercial and Financial Chronicle* was even more critical that the *Protectionist* of the United States intervention in the Dominican Republic because this periodical feared that war would result from this action. The *Chronicle* opposed using American funds for pulling "the European chestnuts out of the fire," and felt the action was unconstitutional.[36] Both the *Protectionist* and the *Commercial and Financial Chronicle* contended that the Roosevelt extension of the Monroe Doctrine did not help commerce, but merely wasted money and created the possibility of war.

Business desired stability in Latin America, but not at the expense of a loss of trade because of antagonism toward the United States. Thus, commerce opposed the involvement of the

United States in areas where a solution could be found without American aid and subsequent criticism of the United States. The *New York Commercial* expressed its opposition to American intervention into the tangled affairs of Haiti. This newspaper cautioned the United States to act only in an emergency that would menace seriously the Monroe Doctrine, particularly as this country was involved in the domestic affairs of the Philippines, Alaska, Guam, Hawaii, and Cuba.[37] Similarly, the *American Exporter* warned against American interference in Nicaragua.

> Mr. Knox's handling of the Nicaragua incident has already destroyed a portion of Mr. Root's work of building up a cordial feeling of friendship between the Latin American countries and the United States. Our exchanges show that even some of the most powerful and level headed of South American republics are nursing extreme irritation over the manner in which the United States Department of State interferred with Zelaya. This is to be deeply regretted. Latin America has a very strong suspicion, albeit unfounded, of our intentions toward it in general, and it behooves us to allay that suspicion at every opportunity, not add to it.[38]

Business took every opportunity it could to alleviate the fears of Latin America over the intentions of the United States. Thus, the *Protectionist* criticized the jingoist newspapers for advocating territorial acquisitions by the United States in Central and South America. This kind of discussion, the *Protectionist* warned, had created distrust in South America of the United States, thus enabling European nations to use this fear to cripple trade with the United States.[39] The *Journal of Commerce* wished that Latin America would understand the true intentions of the United States, which were peaceful. All that it desired was an enlightened sisterhood of American states, independent and self-governing. The United States did not want to do anything more than to protect those countries from the encroachments of Europe while they tried to solve their own problems.[40]

While there was a difference of opinion among businessmen over the wisdom of a general policy of interference in Latin American affairs, there was agreement that the United States had a special responsibility toward Cuba, due to the prominent role played by the United States in bringing about the island's independence. American capitalists also had substantial investments there which would be endangered if Cuba followed the pattern of other southern nations in her relations with foreign businessmen. Charles Conant wrote, during the 1907 intervention, that the United States had a greater responsibility in Cuba than the maintenance of order. He urged that after the troops were withdrawn, the United States should exercise a strong control over the legislative and financial affairs of that country in order to prevent a lapse into anarchy. Conant considered the mass of Cuban people unfit for self-government and a threat to the conservative business class of the country who desired American control. He contended that the United States must play a large role in the improvement and maintenance of the Cuban nation.[41]

Conant's views were largely shared by the *Journal of Commerce*. This newspaper concluded that since the United States had fought a war with Spain because of the latter's inability to maintain order in Cuba, America had a responsibility toward upholding harmony in Cuba after the war had been won. The *Journal of Commerce* also reminded its readers that the United States had invested in Cuba 150 million dollars which would be lost if Cuban internal affairs became chaotic. The newspaper hoped that United States soldiers would be removed from the island, but that precautions against another uprising would be taken. These safeguards should be in the form of a low sugar tariff, the *Journal* contended.[42]

Financial Age saw intervention in Cuba as being necessary for the protection of the funds invested there, but it balked at the calling of a special Congressional session to appropriate funds for the undertaking, and suggested instead, that the Marines be immediately withdrawn.[43]

There was little desire on the part of business to annex Cuba. The *Wall Street Journal* believed that no policy of the United States had brought it more credit than its Cuban policy. America had given Cuba its independence, a stable government, and needed reform measures. Annexation was contrary to the will of the United States and talk of the matter only created suspicion toward America. The position of the United States was that of an elder brother to Latin America. The United States because of its power was almost sovereign over the entire territory. This involved a duty to maintain peace and order there.[44]

The *Protectionist*, which also favored an independent status for Cuba, contended:

> Cuban independence is desirable, not only for our own interests, but for those of the island. Annexation and the rule of the island as a colony or dependent territory can come only as a result of the complete demonstration of the inability of the islanders to conduct their own political affairs.[45]

Business, then, could not be classified with those interest groups which favored Cuban territorial aggrandizement. Most businessmen's views were similar to those of the *Wall Street Journal* and the *Protectionist* which disclaimed any right of the United States to occupy Cuba, although both periodicals believed that intervention in the affairs of Cuba to maintain peace was justified.

Those businessmen who had an interest in Latin America were primarily concerned with trade. Since Latin America was richer and closer to the United States than Asia, quite a few leaders of commerce were concerned that the United States had not captured a greater share of this southern market. Failure to enter this market on a greater scale, they believed, would be disastrous to the United States with its increasing industrial surplus. Thus, the only interest businessmen had in Latin America was to seek ways and means of enlarging this potential market. These businessmen were not interested in increasing the number of American possessions. Rather, they were opposed to such an expansion in Latin America because it disturbed trade, cost money, and increased Latin American antagonisms toward the United States. Yet many businessmen supported intervention by their government to protect them from hostile Latin American dictators. Moreover, they also favored United States intervention in the Caribbean to maintain that region's stability.

5 | BUSINESS' ATTITUDE TOWARD PEACE

During the decade and a half preceeding World War I, there was an interest in measures aimed at promoting future peace. Americans participated in this movement by attending international peace meetings, by forming national peace societies, and by promoting governmental policies favorable to the pacific settlement of disputes. With the possible exception of the clergy, probably no group in American society contributed more to this movement than did business.

There was more business commentaries on methods of promoting international harmony than on most other areas of foreign policy. Many important leaders of commerce expressed strong opinions in favor of the peace movement. The leading trade associations and chambers of commerce passed many resolutions praising the work of the peace organizations. Moreover, Andrew Carnegie, the universally acknowledged leader of the peace movement until his death, organized the Carnegie Endowment for International Peace, an organization that played a leading role in the breakdown of the American policy of isolation and in the movement to eliminate war.

Businessmen admitted that their contributions to the peace movements were selfishly motivated. Marcus Markes, president of the National Association of Clothiers, contended that without peace commerce could not exist.[1]

For commerce . . . depends upon the stability of government and the friendly relations between nations for the uninterrupted and profitable exchange to the fullest extent. The fact is recognized that only such nations as are in peaceful and friendly contact can thoroughly, sympathetically and satisfactorily study and supply each other's wants, thus developing mutual trading most successfully.

Even a war in which the United States was not involved could have a disastrous result on business. James Van Cleave, president of the National Association of Manufacturers, described the effect of the Russo-Japanese War upon American commerce. During the war, American sales to China, Russia, and Japan increased, but afterwards, the drain of the war upon their resources caused these countries to reduce drastically their imports. Such disruptions of trade were important because they interfered with the efforts of American industry to dispose of its overproduction.[2] A number of businessmen blamed the panic of 1907 on the slowdown of American exports following the Russo-Japanese War.

Many businessmen believed that war was the antithesis of commerce. "War never created wealth as does commerce, instead it fosters an inflation, encourages political corruption and also creates a false prosperity which soon collapses. The immense sums which are diverted from commercial enterprises for military establishments is a heavy tax on business and retards prosperity."[3] Moreover, business learned what could result from an armed conflict by recalling the effects of the Civil War on commerce. One outcome of this war was the destruction of the merchant marine, which as late as 1910 had still not regained its pre-Civil War strength. The mere absence of war at a given time, however, was not enough to satisfy business, according to the *Wall Street Journal*. Business must see far enough ahead into the future to make broad plans. To guarantee a favorable atmosphere for business, all the obstacles to the peaceful progress of nations must be eliminated.[4]

In addition to these contentions that peace was a prerequisite to the development of commerce, many leaders felt that trade was one of the universal forces for peace. John Crosby Brown said that the greater the economic interests that different peoples of the world have at stake in other parts of the globe, the greater the bond of peace binding the world together.[5] Industrial trusts were praised by one leader as among the most important business bonds which produced peace and contended that Morgan's merger of the Atlantic steamship lines was an excellent example of this. Trade was denationalized by centralizing control of commercial avenues. Such mergers, it was thought, put an end to international commercial rivalries, "and put a decided check on that form of national rivalry which takes the shape of armed aggression."[6]

Because of the vast amounts of capital needed to conduct wars, international bankers tried to use their influence to aid the preservation of peace. Isaac Seligman pointed out that the banker was the servant of commerce and that when its free flow was prevented by war, the banker suffered greatly. For this reason, he continued, bankers would scrutinize more carefully bonds floated for military purposes than those floated for peaceful uses.[7] Henry Clews believed that if bankers were consulted before governments declared war, the financial leaders would probably prevent "unnecessary" wars.[8] The classic example of the influence bankers could exert for peace was their success in ending the Russo-Japanese War. They simply refused to make further loans to the participants.

Another indication of business interest in peace was the activity of the International Congress of Chambers of Commerce and Industrial Associations, which met semiannually after 1905. At an initial meeting of the Congress, Harry Wheeler, president of the United States Chamber of Commerce, stated:

> The business interests of the United States are deeply sensible of the importance of this great gathering. It signifies to us a recognition of a world interdependence, an acknowledgement that the happiness, the welfare and the prosperity of the people are so interlaced that harm permitted to be done to the least of the nations must necessarily find its adverse effect upon the greatest.[9]

Some members of the business community did not agree that the cause of peace was improved best by international commercial interdependence. The *Protectionist* declared that the best way to "secure a permanent world peace would be for every nation to mind its own business and avoid foreign entanglements." This periodical contended that since the United States was economically self-sufficient, it could implement its desire for peace by withdrawing from world commercial competition and by raising tariffs. This philosophy was in sharp conflict with those American businessmen who believed that America was overproducing.[10]

A number of business leaders maintained that commerce, which is organized for essentially selfish ends, could not promote

50

international harmony. A New York businessman, in illustrating this opinion, pointed out that during the Civil War both sides were economically independent and northern and southern businessmen were equally opposed to the war. "We see there, I think, an instance of the fact that when people are moved by great moral passion, the commercial interests, selfish as they are, cannot stand against it."[11]

Businessmen feared war for two reasons: (1) because they believed, as indicated above, that in a commercially interdependent world, war would wreck United States commerce; (2) because war was expensive and business bore most of the tax burden. They objected, therefore, to the cost of maintaining a military establishment. In the early part of the twentieth century, the United States was increasing its outlay for military purposes, particularly for the navy. Andrew Carnegie, the outstanding business opponent of large expenditures for military purposes, charged that the United States was spending $300 million a year against an imaginary enemy. Because the country had no enemies, he contended, it needed neither an army nor a navy. Carnegie disputed Roosevelt's declaration that America's strongest defense was a strong offense.[12]

A. B. Farquhar, a leading member of the National Association of Manufacturers and the United States Chamber of Congress, agreed with Carnegie. Farquhar observed that because the United States had no enemies, the country's military preparations appeared to the outside world, and particularly to the Latin American nations, as preliminaries to an aggressive war. He also noted that there were few poorer investments than modern warships, especially since the Russo-Japanese War had shown how easily they could be destroyed. Farquhar maintained that the best policy for the United States was aimed at building up the country's resources and discharging its debts.[13]

Marcus Markes also disputed Roosevelt's claim that peace could best be maintained by preparedness. Markes believed that a million dollars spent in the cause of peace would do more for the maintenance of world order than ten million dollars spent on armaments.[14]

Other business leaders disagreed with Carnegie and those who shared his views. These spokesmen felt that before disarmament could take place, some measure to maintain peace had to be devised. Businessmen at the Lake Mohonk Conference on Arbitration resolved that only when international arbitration was substituted for war as a means of settling international disputes could the burden of armaments be lifted from industry and commerce.[15] The *Commercial and Financial Chronicle* observed that the nations of the world would bring financial ruin upon themselves unless they reduced their armies, but this periodical did not consider disarmament a practical solution to the dilemma.[16] Henry Clews also contended that since the disarmament of nations "is grand in theory, but not practical at present," the United States, in order to insure peace, had to prepare for war. The United States would then be so strong that no other nation would dare attack.[17]

Most businessmen considered arbitration as the best means of obtaining peace and gave unqualified support to agencies promoting arbitration. The New York Chamber of Commerce, for example, consistently advocated mediating international disputes, particularly those arising between the United States and England, such as the Venezuelan boundary dispute.[18] Because of their interest in this method of promoting peace, businessmen played a prominent role in the formation of the Lake Mohonk Conference on Arbitration. The Conference, created to promote world peace through arbitration, devoted one session at its annual meeting to the opinions of business leaders on this subject. By 1913, almost all of the major American business organizations were represented at the Conference. The total number of business organizations participating in the Conference was one hundred and seventy-seven, including six national business groups.[19] At the 1903 Conference, a special committee composed of businessmen stated the reasons why mercantile interests favored arbitration. The committee contended that because war disrupts commerce and brings disaster to business, armed conflicts must be avoided without submitting the parties to dishonor or injustice. Arbitration was not only a practical way to accomplish this, but it also removed effectively the desire for war. If nations knew that disputes would be arbitrated, armaments would be reduced, thus lessening further the possibility of war.[20]

Most of the major business organizations of the United States had committees devoted to the promotion of mediation. Those groups without such committees usually discussed arbitration at annual meetings. The National Board of Trade, for example, resolved at its 1907 meeting that the efforts which had been made to secure arbitration of international disputes be recognized as promoting the highest degree of civilization. The continuation of these efforts was commended by the Board as being in the interest of present and later generations of mankind.[21]

Although there was little business opposition to arbitration, there was some skepticism as to whether it could prevent all wars. The president of the Merchants Association of New York believed that the free exchange of goods among nations was a prerequisite to successful arbitration. If the United States wanted mediation established on a firm basis to prevent war, it must be willing also to work for reciprocity in order to eliminate mutual distrust.[22] A business delegate to the Lake Mohonk Conference contended that arbitration had definite limitations. He said that there were many disputes between nations which could only be settled by war. This is especially true "where nations are claiming rights which they are meaning to take in spite of all law and justice."[23] The *Journal of Commerce* noted that national ambition was more of a cause of war than international misunderstandings. Consequently, the only way to control national ambition was to strengthen the weaker nations so that they could resist aggression.[24]

Business supported the arbitration treaties negotiated by the United States with England and France, for they provided a way of settling disputes without disrupting trade. Many organizations of businessmen put pressure on the Senate to accept the treaties and to urge the State Department to conclude similar ones with other nations.[25] The business committee of the Lake Mohonk Conference urged business leaders to influence the Senate to ratify the treaties without amendments, for in the past so many exceptions had been included in these arbitration treaties that they were made worthless. The treaties with Great Britain and France provided for the arbitration of all possible disputes. "If they are altered in the Senate," the Conference maintained, "the world will consider it a defeat, more or less, of the undertaking, and thus . . . injury will result."[26]

Although bilateral arbitration treaties were considered useful, businessmen active in the peace movement thought that nothing less than a general court of arbitration could preserve international harmony. Thus, they supported the Hague Conference and the Hague Court of Arbitration. *The Banker's Magazine* noted that the end of a war does not assure that an international dispute has been settled with due fairness to the parties involved. The creation of an international court, on the other hand, would promote justice in such conflicts. This financial journal also expressed hope that the Hague Conference of 1906, by creating a more peaceful atmosphere, would give the great powers of the world the opportunity to relieve themselves of the financial burdens of maintaining large armies.[27] When critics of the Hague Conference questioned its worth, A. B. Farquhar defended it by contending that the greatest accomplishment of the meeting was the fact that the governments of the world over had held a gathering dedicated to peace. Farquhar hoped that a third meeting at the Hague would lead to a permanent organization.[28]

The National Board of Trade was not satisfied with either the Hague Conference or the Hague Court. It represented many groups of businessmen when it urged President Roosevelt to use his influence to have the Hague Conference created into a permanent congress of nations with advisory powers.[29] Andrew Carnegie had a similar proposal in his League of Peace idea. Carnegie wanted the United States, Great Britain, and Germany to form a new triple entente. Since these nations were the most important industrial and commercial nations in the world, they had the most to gain from the maintenance of peace. Proof that these nations could enforce their decisions against those who sought to break the peace was furnished by the Boxer Rebellion. By cooperating in this instance, these three nations were able to bring peace to the Chinese mainland. They could do the same thing any where else in the world.[30] *Iron Age,* in agreeing with Carnegie, commented:

> If three or four of the leading powers — as, for instance, Great Britain, Germany, and the United States — could be persuaded to unite in a plan to compel the preservation of the peace of the world through the Hague Conference or some similar organization, it would seem highly probable that the other great powers would join them and the rest of the world would follow.[31]

Henry Clews also advocated the creation of a League for Peace, but he contended, Japan should be in the partnership with Britain and the United States. No peace alliance, Clews maintained, could be considered complete without a representative from the Far East. He went on to say, as others did, that if these nations worked together, the other major countries would have to join.[32] Business leaders proposed the creation of an organization for the maintenance of peace strikingly similar to the concept embodied in the charters of the League of Nations and the United Nations. The Councils in both organizations were to perform a function patterned after the League of Peace concept.

Businessmen such as Carnegie and Clews were in favor of some type of organizaton to prevent war because they believed that armed conflict was a threat to commerce. They participated with other groups in the Lake Mohonk Conference on Arbitration and in the American Peace Congress and consequently made valuable contributions to the peace movement. Since large armaments meant high taxes, businessmen generally opposed military preparedness. For this reason, they supported methods of preserving peace that would eliminate the threat of war altogether and so put an end to the need for large armies. Arbitration and the judicial settlement of disputes would create the atmosphere which they hoped would achieve their ends.

Because the average businessman regarded peace as the cornerstone of economic prosperity, the outbreak of war in Europe on August 1, 1914, one month after the assassination of Archduke Franz Ferdinand of Austria, came as a particularly bitter shock.[33] As had been long suspected by American business leaders, the opening of hostilities was almost as commercially disastrous for the United States as it was for each of the belligerents. The great interdependence of the industrial nations of the world meant that even neutrality by the United States would not prevent a serious disruption of the American economy.

Since nothing disturbs the investor more than future uncertainty, the first major economic consequence of the war was a collapse of stock prices. General Motors, for example, fell from $83 to $53 a share, American Smelting from $69 to $52, while United States Steel fell from $59 to $51 during several days of hectic trading preceeding the formal opening of the war.[34] To prevent a complete selloff, the New York Stock Exchange remained closed between July 30 and December 11, during which time member firms were prohibited from dealing in listed securities.[35]

American exports and imports were also paralyzed by the opening of hostilities. Orders canceled by the belligerents piled up at Eastern seaboard ports while Midwestern and Southern industrialists decided what to do with their goods.[36] Trade figures for September, 1914, as compared to September, 1913, illustrate the immediate impact of the war. The value of all American exports declined in value from two hundred million dollars to one hundred and fifty million dollars.[37] War also resulted in shortages of merchant ships, of dye stuffs, and of chemicals heretofore produced by Germany for American manufacturers.[38]

55

The severe economic recession which followed this disruption of normal economic relations resulted in almost seventeen thousand business failures during 1914, one of the highest figures in American history.[39] A severe unemployment also developed especially in the East.[40]

This experience in 1914 left most businessmen convinced that war brought only disaster to finance, commerce, and industry, and that whatever profits might be made later would not compensate for the losses already incurred.[41] The animosity of business towards war was not weakened by the massive military purchases by the Allies in the United States beginning in the spring of 1915. Although a number of "war securities" reached all time high prices, many business journals looked upon this prosperity as a mirage which would disappear as soon as the European War was over with dire results for the whole economy.[42]

Because they opposed all wars, businessmen were particularly in favor of maintaining American neutrality in the European conflict.[43] Their general feeling was that only by remaining neutral would the United States retain its prosperity and hence be in a position to aid in the reconstruction of the world at the end of the war.[44] Thus, despite the opposition of most businessmen to President Wilson's domestic policy, they supported his declaration of American neutrality.[45] After the German destruction of the *Lusitania,* the President received business's unanimous support in his stand against the German use of the submarine. One of Wilson's most persistant business critics wrote that every American stood behind him in his determination to make, "Kaiser Wilhelm regard the rights of Americans on the high seas, and cease his deliberate murder of innocent women and children and unarmed men, as in his hellish way in sinking the *Lusitania.*"[46]

Business support for neutrality was supplemented by a continued connection with the peace movement. Representatives from trade and commercial associations were present at the last two Lake Mohonk Conferences on International Arbitration in 1915 and 1916.[47] However, the magnitude of the European war revealed the inadequacy of international arbitration as a means of preventing wars. New solutions to this problem were sought by the businessmen who helped to form the Society to Eliminate the Economic Causes of War and the League to Enforce the Peace.[48] The proposals of the League, which included participation by the United States in a Council of Conciliation with the power to use economic and military sanctions against members who threatened the peace, were patterned after ideas advocated by Andrew Carnegie before the war.[49]

It was this passionate desire for peace by most of the business community which led to the abortive effort by Henry Ford to end the war in 1915. Deeply disturbed by the European struggle, the Detroit automobile manufacturer refused to accept war orders.[50] Ford, deciding in the fall of 1915 that if the war did not end immediately the United States would become involved, financed a peace mission to Europe by prominent Americans aboard the Peace Ship. This mission was to be the prelude to a general conference of neutral nations designed to apply moral pressure to bring the war to a close.[51] When the mission failed after two months in Europe to end the war, Ford established the Neutral Conference for Continuous Mediation, with several paid directors who remained in Europe during 1916.[52] The Ford Peace Mission might easily be described as the action of an eccentric millionaire. But this generalization overlooks the fact that this scheme developed out of the pre-war business conviction that peace might be achieved through arbitration.

Although the vast majority of American businessmen had opposed the entrance by the United States into the war, this did not prevent them from taking sides in the struggle or from urging the rebuilding of American defenses. Like most other Americans, businessmen were pro-Allied, because of the great cultural and economic ties between the United States and England and because of a hostility towards Germany that antedated the war.[53] Pro-Allied sentiment continued to be expressed throughout the struggle and did not increase substantially after England and France began their purchases in the United States.

While disturbed by the high costs of armaments, the commercial, financial, and industrial interests of the United States accepted the need for an adequate American defense.[54] To promote this preparedness, a number of business leaders organized the National Security League in December, 1914, in New York City.[55] The League called for an increase in the size of the army from its peacetime strength of 200,000 soldiers to one million men and for a buildup of the navy.[56] A poll of bankers in Illinois by *The Bankers Magazine* is probably typical of business sentiment in the country. Five hundred and sixty-two of those polled favored military and naval preparedness while only twenty-eight opposed preparedness.[57] In their attitude towards preparedness, it is quite likely that these business leaders were motivated not only by a desire for national security, but also by a desire for the profits that would come their way.[58]

There is no doubt that the vast expansion of the war industries did mitigate the hostility of a segment of the business community towards war. But there is no reason to believe what Walter Millis and C. C. Tansill asserted in the 1930's, that business wanted war.[59] Until December, 1916, the loans made by American bankers to England and France were guaranteed by high grade collateral pledged by the Allies. There was no danger to this collateral even if an Allied collapse occurred on the battlefield.[60] The legend that the business community desired war does not hold up even under the most superficial examination.[61]

Businessmen, like almost every other segment of American public opinion, were pushed towards a desire for war only after the all out German submarine campaign began on January 31, 1917. Until that time, little, if any, open desire for war existed.

SUMMARY

In the first decade of the twentieth century, a group of American intellectual and commercial leaders were committed to the idea that their country was producing more than it could consume. These men were convinced that unless American industrial surpluses were reduced both the political and economic stability of the United States were threatened. One practical method of preventing this internal disaster was to use American foreign policy as a tool to rid the United States of its surplus. This could be done by having the government use its influence to open markets for American products.

Because of this desire for new markets, American business leaders were particularly interested in China. The Spanish-American War had resulted in the acquisition of the Philippines, a base close to China. Thus, the United States had access to millions of potential customers. To facilitate a speedy exploitation of the Chinese market, the leaders of the business community first proposed the building of a Central American canal, the laying of a trans-Pacific cable, and building up the American merchant marine. Threats to China's integrity seemed to negate America's new found advantage. For this reason, business gave warm support to the Open Door Policy. Subsequently, when Russia appeared to be the threat to the American markets in Manchuria, business supported Japan in the Russo-Japanese War.

After this war a number of businessmen grew apprehensive of Japan's new position in the Far East. The Harriman and Schiff attempt to gain control of the Manchurian railroads, for example, was an effort to thwart Japan's ambitions in that area. Under American control these railroads could have been used to keep Manchuria open to trade from the United States. When Harriman and his colleagues failed to neutralize the Manchurian railroads, the American government attempted to accomplish the same end through the banking consortium. Although this venture also failed to introduce American railroads into China, Manchuria was still open to American products in 1914. It is problematic whether this was achieved by American effort or some other force, such as the growing crisis in Europe.

Many business men such as John Hays Hammond and Charles Conant believed that an increased trade in Asia was not sufficient, but that the United States also had to take a greater interest in Latin America. These men warned that if the United States did not exploit this potentially large market, it would discover that it had been excluded from it by England and Germany. When the Latin American market would be needed to take up the industrial surplus, it would be gone. In order to promote a buildup of trade with Latin America, the government was urged to give the same type of protection England and Germany provided for their enterpreneurs. If threatened by a local dictator, the American businessman wanted to be sure that his government would use its power in his behalf. Other businessmen also believed that the United States had to maintain the stability of neighboring Caribbean states. This was necessary to protect the many American investors there and also to prevent the European countries from exploiting Latin America's political instability. Despite the attention devoted to increasing Latin American trade by such groups as the National Association of Manufacturers, there was no substantial growth during this period. There was, however, a rapid increase in American investments in the Western Hemisphere, especially in Mexico and the Caribbean area.

Although the greater part of the trade of the United States was with Europe, there was little vocal business comment on European affairs. When a European monarch died, or when an internal political upheaval occurred, such as the Russian Revolution of 1905, the business periodicals would devote some editorial comment to it. Otherwise, the major crisis in Europe received much less attention than similar events in Latin America or

Asia. Perhaps this silence was due to the traditional American apprehension of European affairs, or it might have been due to the idea that in the future Latin America or Asia would be more important as markets to the United States than Europe. The United States by 1900 was in direct competition with Europe for the markets of the backwards areas. Many businessmen believed that for this reason a decline in American trade with Europe was to be expected.

Business was concerned with the political instability of Europe as a great threat to the peace. To assure continued American prosperity and to rid itself of its surplus there had to be peace. Thus many businessmen contributed heavily to the peace movement. To these businessmen, war meant added taxes, a greater degree of government control, and social unrest, perhaps even the development of socialism. There were, naturally, groups of businesses that could hope to prosper by war, but, especially among commercial representatives of business, war was the opposite of what they hoped to achieve. The interests of businessmen in the peace movement is evidenced by the major role they played at every peace conference.

In retrospect, the business fear that the American economy would collapse if it did not export a greater percentage of its industrial output because of overproduction seems groundless now. During the whole period, there was little increase in exports, yet the predicted economic collapse did not come about. Even before the First World War, the thesis of overproduction had been attacked by such economists as Veblen. Despite this fact, the belief that the United States was producing more than it could consume was a familiar one after 1914 and was heard quite often during the depression of 1929.

Not only did the fear of overproduction turn out to be unrealistic, but the hope of a great market in China turned out to be a dream. The businessmen who believed that China's three hundred million customers could solve all their problems were following the same Western tradition that led Marco Polo to China and Columbus to the West Indies. This belief in China did not die with the First World War, but continued into the 1920's and 1930's.

On the other hand Latin America developed into an important United States market. Although by 1920, the United States still bought more from Latin America than it sold, this trend was soon reversed. Moreover, the Western Hemisphere continued to be the most important area of American investments. The basis

61

of a lucrative market in that area was laid partially as a result of the theory of overproduction which so concerned business opinion during the first decade of the twentieth century.

BIBLIOGRAPHY

BOOKS AND PAMPHLETS

Adams, Brooks. *America's Economic Supremacy.* New York, 1900.

Beal, Howard K. *Theodore Roosevelt and the Rise of America to World Power.* Baltimore, 1956.

Blakeslee, George H., ed. *Latin America. Clark University Addresses.* New York, 1914.

—————————————, ed. *Recent Developments in China. Clark University Addresses.* New York, 1913.

Campbell, Charles. *Special Business Interests and the Open Door Policy.* New Haven, 1951.

Carnegie, Andrew. *Address by Andrew Carnegie at the Fourth American Peace Conference, St. Louis, 1913.* New York, 1913.

Clews, Henry. *An Address Delivered at the Banquet Given in Honor of the President of the United States by the American Peace and Arbitration League, March 22, 1910.* New York, 1910.

Conant, Charles A. *The United States and the Orient: The Nature of the Economic Problem.* Boston, 1900.

Croly, Herbert. *Willard Straight.* New York, 1924.

Dodsworth, William. *Our Industrial Position and Our Policy in the Pacific.* New York, 1898.

Dunn, Robert. *American Foreign Investments.* New York, 1926.

Ginger, Ray. *Age of Excess: the United States from 1877 to 1914.* New York, 1965.

Harrison, F. C. and Conant, Charles A. *Monetary Reform for Nicaragua: Submitted to Messers Brown Brothers and J. W. Seligman and Company.* New York, 1912.

Kennan, George. *Edward Harriman.* 2 vols. New York, 1922.

Kennan, George F. *American Diplomacy: 1900-1950.* New York, 1952.

Kepner, Charles David and Soothill, Jay Henry. *The Banana Empire: A Case Study of Economic Imperialism.* New York, 1935.

Kirkland, Edward C. *Dream and Thought in the Business Community, 1860-1900.* Ithaca, New York, 1956.

Millard, Thomas F. *America and the Far Eastern Question.* New York, 1909.

Mills, Walter. *Road to War: America, 1914-1917.* Boston, 1935.

Morgan, H. Wayne. *America's Road to Empire: The War with Spain and Overseas Expansion.* New York, 1965.

New York and Bermudez Company. *The Seizure of the Property of the New York and Bermudez Company by the Venezuelan Government: A Statement by the Company.* New York, 1906.

New York Commercial. Santo Domingo, A Brief Sketch of the Island, Its Resources and Commercial Possibilities with Special Reference to the Treaty Now Pending in the United States Senate. New York, 1906.

Norton, Henry Kittridge. *China and the Powers.* New York, 1927.

Pratt, Julius William. *Expansionists of 1898.* Baltimore, 1936.

Ridgeway, George L. *Merchants of Peace: Thirty Years of Business Diplomacy Through the International Chamber of Commerce, 1919-1938.* New York, 1938.

Rippy, Fred J. *The Capitalists and Colombia.* New York, 1931.

Russell, Lord Lindsay. *America to Japan: A Symposium of Papers by Representative Citizens of the United States of America on the Common Interests of the Two Countries.* New York, 1914.

Steigerwalt, Albert. *The National Association of Manufacturers, 1895-1915: A Study in Business Leadership* ("Michigan Business Studies," Vol. XVI, No. 2.) Grand Rapids, 1964.

Tansill, Charles C. *America Goes to War.* Boston, 1938.

Tupper, Eleanor and McReynolds, George E. *Japan in American Public Opinion.* New York, 1937.

Vevier, Charles. *The United States and China, 1906-1913: A Study of Finance and Diplomacy.* New Brunswick, 1955.

Williams, William A. *The Tragedy of American Foreign Policy.* Cleveland, 1959.

Zabriskie, Edward H. *American Russian Rivalry in the Far East: A Study in Diplomacy and Power Politics, 1895-1914.* Philadelphia, 1946.

ARTICLES

[Annon.] "Corollaries of Expansion: I The Nicaragua Canal." *Literary Digest,* XX (Feb. 10, 1900), 177-178.

[Annon.] "Corollaries of Expansion: II Shipping Subsidies." *Literary Digest,* XX (Feb. 17, 1900), 205-207.

Atkinson, Edward. "Eastern Commerce: What Is It Worth?" *North American Review,* CLXX (Feb., 1900), 295-304.

Barrett, John. "America in China: Our Position and Opportunity," *North American Review*, CLXXV (Nov., 1902), 655-663.

Carnegie, Andrew. "American Expansion," *American Iron and Steel Association Bulletin*, III (Oct. 15, 1900), 171-173.

Clews, Henry. "England and Russia in Our Civil War," *North American Review*, CLXXVIII (June, 1904), 812-819.

—————————, "The Economics of Peace," *The Peace Forum*, II (May, 1914), 43.

Conant, Charles A. "Our Duty in Cuba," *North American Review*, CLXXV May, 1907), 141-146.

Hammond, John Hays. "American Commercial Interests in the Far East," *Annals of the American Academy of Political and Social Science*, XXVI (July, 1905), 85-88.

Miller, Warner, "The Meaning of the Isthmanian Canal," *American Industries*, I (April 15, 1903), 1-2.

Pratt, Sereno S. "The Contribution of Commerce to International Unity," *International Conciliation*, No. 50 (Jan., 1912), 5-18.

Seligman, Isaac, "International Banking and Its Important Influence on International Unity," *International Conciliation*, No. 50 (Jan., 1912), 19-30.

Syrett, Harold. "The Business Press and American Neutrality, 1914-1917," *The Mississippi Valley Historical Review*, XXXII (Sept., 1945), 215-230.

Thorson, Winston B. "American Public Opinion and the Portsmouth Conference," *American Historical Review*, LIII (April, 1948), 439-464.

NEWSPAPERS AND PERIODICALS

Advocate of Peace. 1910-1916.
American Banker. 1900-1917.
American Industries. 1902-1912.
American Iron and Steel Association Bulletin. 1900-1916.
Asia: Journal of the American Asiatic Society. 1894-1914.
Bradstreet's. 1900-1910.
Commercial America. 1904-1912.
Commercial and Financial Chronicle. 1900-1917.
Financial Age. 1900-1916.
Iron Age. 1900-1912.
Marine Journal. 1900-1907.
New York Commercial. 1901-1912.
New York Journal of Commerce and Commercial Bulletin. 1903-1912.
New York Wall Street Journal. 1901-1917.
San Francisco Merchants Association Review. 1907-1911.
Textile World. 1900-1905.
The Banker's Magazine. 1900-1917.
The New York Times. 1910-1917.
The Protectionist. 1900-1917.

REPORTS AND PROCEEDINGS

Chamber of Commerce of New York State. *Annual Report,* 1900-1913.

Lake Mohonk Conference on International Arbitration. *Report of Annual Meeting,* 1900-1916.

National Arbitration and Peace Congress. *Proceedings.* New York, 1907.

National Association of Cotton Manufacturers. *Transactions of Annual Meeting,* 1906-1913.

National Association of Manufacturers. *Proceedings of Annual Convention,* 1900-1914.

————————. In Cooperation with Banking and Transportation Interests of the United States. *Proceedings of the International Trade Conference.* New York, 1915.

National Board of Trade. *Proceedings of Annual Meeting,* 1900-1911.

New England Cotton Manufacturers' Association. *Report of the Annual Meeting,* 1900-1906.

Philadelphia Board of Trade. *Annual Report,* 1900-1910.

PUBLIC DOCUMENTS

U.S. Senate Documents, 60 Cong., 1 Sess (1908), XXIV, No. 413.

U.S. Senate, Subcommittee of the Committee on Interstate Commerce. *Hearing on Resolution S. No. 139, Submitted by Mr. Johnston, Directing the Department of Commerce and Labor to Make an Investigation into the Character and Operations of the United Fruit Company.* Series No. 8, 60 Cong., 1 Sess., April 22, 1908.

NOTES

1 | THE THESIS OF OVERPRODUCTION

1. William Dodsworth was an editor of the *Journal of Commerce;* Brooks Adams, a brother of Henry Adams, wrote extensively on industry and civilization; Charles Conant, who was a prominent banker and an officer of the American Bankers' Association, wrote a number of books on business and finance.

2. William Dodsworth, *Our Industrial Position and Our Policy in the Pacific* (New York, 1900), p. 3. For an historical analysis of the problem of overproduction and its influence on public policy see Ray Ginger, *Age of Excess, The United States from 1877 to 1914* (New York, 1965) and Walter Le Feber, *The New Empire* (Ithaca, 1963).

3. Charles Conant. *The United States and the Orient: The Nature of the Economic Problem* (Boston, 1900), p. 5.

4. J. M. Thompson, speech, in the New England Cotton Manufacturers' Association, *Report of the Annual Meeting* (Boston, 1900), p. 5.

5. Dodsworth, *op. cit.,* p. 5.

6. *Ibid,* p. 6.

7. *Ibid.,* p. 12.

8. Conant, *op. cit.,* pp. 24-26.

9. Theodore C. Search, speech in the National Association of Manufacturers, *Proceedings of the Fifth Annual Convention* (1900), p. 4.

10. Edward Atkinson, "Eastern Commerce: What Is It Worth?" *North American Review,* CLXX (Feb.. 1900), 295.

11. *Textile World,* XIX (Aug., 1900), 224.

12. Frederic Covery, "The Dominant Question," *The Review of the World's Commerce,* reprinted in *Asia, Journal of the American Asiatic Society,* I (Aug. 25, 1898), p. 8.

13. Among the advertisers in *Asia* were During Milliken & Co., Faulkner Page & Co., Eldridge, Lewes & Co., E. D. Cerdes & Co., and Joshua Bailey & Co., all of whom were manufacturers or distributors of cotton goods.

14. For a further exploration of American business interest in the Orient after the Spanish American War, see Charles Campbell, *Special Business Interests and the Open Door Policy* (New Haven, 1951).

15. National Association of Manufacturers, *Proceedings of the Eighth Annual Convention* (1903), p. 77.

16. Andrew Carnegie, "American Expansion," *American Iron and Steel Association Bulletin,* XIV, (Oct. 15, 1900), 172.

17. *American Banker, LXVI* (Jan. 19, 1901), 150.

18. *Ibid.*

19. *United States Investor,* XVII (Jan. 27, 1906), 140.

20. John Barrett, "America in China: Our Position and Opportunity." *North American Review,* CLXXV (Oct., 1902), 68.

21. Resolution of the Southern Cotton Spinners Association, reprinted in *Asia,* I (Nov. 13, 1899), 68.

22. National Association of Manufacturers, *Proceedings of the Eighth Annual Convention* (1903), p. 70.

23. Warner Miller. "The Meaning of the Isthmanian Canal," *American Industries,* I (April 15, 1903), 2.

24. National Association of Manufacturers, *Proceedings of the Eighth Annual Convention* (1903), p. 75.

25. *Iron Age, LXVI* (Dec. 20, 1900), 28.

26. *Ibid.*

27. "Corollaries of Expansion," I The Nicaragua Canal," *Literary Digest,* XX (Feb. 10, 1900), 178.

28. *American Iron and Steel Association Bulletin,* XXIV (Feb. 15, 1900), 36.

29. *Commercial and Financial Chronicle,* LXXI (Dec. 20, 1900), 1242.

30. *Ibid.,* LXXVII (Nov. 28, 1903), 2073.

31. *Iron Age, LXVI* (Nov. 22, 1900), 28.

32. *Ibid.,* LXV (Jan. 4, 1900), 39.

33. National Association of Manufacturers, *Proceedings of the Ninth Annual Convention* (1904), p. 170.

34. "Corollaries of Expansion, II Shipping Subsidies," *Literary Digest,* XX (Feb. 17, 1900), 206.

35. National Board of Trade, *Proceedings of the Thirty-First Annual Meeting* (1901), pp. 146-151.

36. *American Iron and Steel Association Bulletin,* XXIV (Feb. 1, 1900), 28.

37. Campbell, *op. cit.,* p. 62.

38. National Association of Manufacturers, *Proceedings of the Ninth Annual Convention* (1904), 105.

2 | THE OPEN DOOR AND AFTERWARDS

1. Charles Vevier, *The United States and China, 1906-1913: A Study of Finance and Diplomacy* (New Brunswick, 1955), p. 92.

2. Business based its fear that any annexations by Europeans of Chinese territory would lead to an exclusion of American goods on its experience with the French in Madagascar. One year after the French annexed the island, the value of American imports there dropped from $431,688 to $2,245. Charles A. Campbell, *Special Business Interests and the Open Door Policy* (New Haven, 1951), p. 21.

3. *Ibid.,* p. 45.

4. New England Cotton Manufacturers Association, *Transactions of the Sixty-ninth Semiannual Meeting* (1900), p. 292.

5. *Asia,* I (June 10, 1899), 53-54.

6. *Iron Age,* LXIX (June 2, 1902), 18.

7. *Asia,* I (March 17, 1900), 81.

8. *Commercial and Financial Chronicle,* LXXXI (July, 1905), 124.

9. *Asia,* I (June, 1900), 100.

10. George F. Kennan, *American Diplomacy: 1900-1950* (New York, 1952) treats critically the term Open Door as an unrealistic term which should not have been applied to foreign business activity in China from 1900 on. Because these business activities in China were, "so complex, so varied, and in many instances so contradictory that no two word formula or symbol could possibly have any plain and comprehensive meaning adequate as a criterion for international agreement on a large number of practical questions."

11. *Asia,* I (October 31, 1898), 14.

12. *American Banker,* LXV (June 20, 1900), 1090.

13. *Ibid.*

14. *Commercial and Financial Chronicle,* LXXI (July 7, 1900), 2.

15. New England Cotton Manufacturers, *Transactions of Sixty-ninth Semiannual Meeting* (1900), p. 323.

16. *Asia,* I (November 26, 1900), 107.

17. John Barrett, "America in China: Our Position and Opportunity," *North American Review,* CLXXXV (Nov., 1902), 655-663.

18. *American Banker,* LXVI (May 18, 1901), 966.

19. *Iron Age,* LXV (Jan. 18, 1900), 22.

20. *Commercial and Financial Chronicle,* LXXVIII (Jan. 30, 1904), 307.

21. *Asia,* IV (Feb., 1904), 1.

22. Henry Clews, "England and Russia in our Civil War," *North American Review,* CLXXXVIII (Jan. 30, 1904), 812-819.

23. Cyrus Adler, *Jacob Schiff — His Life and Letters* (2 vols., Garden City, 1928), II, p. 17.

24. *Commercial and Financial Chronicle*, LXXVII (Nov. 28, 1903), 2067.
25. *American Industries*, X (Sept. 15, 1905), 7.
26. *Commercial and Financial Chronicle*, LXXVII (Feb. 13, 1904), 671.
27. *Asia*, IV (April, 1904), 78.
28. *American Banker*, LXIX.
29. Henry Clews, *op. cit.*, 819.
30. *Commercial and Financial Chronicle*, LXXX (April 22, 1905), 1445.
31. *American Industries*, IV (Sept. 15, 1905), 7.
32. Cyrus Adler, *op. cit.*, pp. 214-217.
33. Edward H. Zabriskie, *American-Russian Rivalry in the Far East, A Study in Diplomacy and Power Politics, 1895-1914* (Philadelphia, 1946), p. 109, footnote 41.
34. *Wall Street Journal*, Feb. 11, 1904.
35. *The Financial Age*, X (August 8, 1904), 262.
36. *The Banker's Magazine*, LXXI (Sept., 1905), 321.
37. *Commercial and Financial Chronicle*, LXXIX (Oct. 29, 1904), 1920.
38. *Asia*, IV (Oct., 1904), 257.
39. *Commercial and Financial Chronicle*, LXXX (March 25, 1904), 1140.
40. *Wall Street Journal*, August 2, 1905.
41. *The Financial Age*, XII (August 21, 1905), 378.
42. *The Banker's Magazine*, LXXI (August, 1905), 147.
43. Winston B. Thorson, "American Public Opinion and the Portsmouth Conference," *American Historical Review*, LIII (April, 1948), 443-444.
44. *American Exporter*, LVI (Sept. 14, 1905), 91.
45. *Iron Age*, LXXVI (Sept. 7, 1905), 616.
46. *Asia*, VII (Sept., 1905), 225.

3 | FAR EASTERN PROBLEMS

1. *Asia*, VI (April, 1906), 75.
2. New York Chamber of Commerce, *Annual Report for 1905-1906* (New York, 1906), p. xi.
3. *Asia*, II (Feb. 8, 1902), 25.
4. *Ibid.*, VII (April 7, 1907), 67. American business was more vocal in its demand for a revision of the Chinese immigration laws than on any other issue in American foreign policy in this period. For other resolutions by business against the Chinese Exclusion Act see: National Board of Trade, *Proceedings of the Thirty-seventh Annual Meeting* (1907), p. 153; Philadelphia Board of Trade, *Seventy-second Annual Report* (1905) p. 440; National Association of Manufacturers, *Proceeding of Ninth Annual Convention* (1904), p. 91.
5. *Asia*, VI (April, 1906), 72.
6. National Board of Trade, *Proceedings of the Thirty-Seventh Annual Meeting* (1907), p. 153.

7. Eleanor Tuper and George E. McReynolds, *Japan in American Public Opinion* (New York, 1937), p. 30, points out that Southern business interests, who had an important need for cheap labor, favored loose immigration laws.

8. Waldo Smith, speech in National Board of Trade, *Proceedings of the Thirty-seventh Annual Meeting* (1907), p. 71.

9. National Association of Cotton Manufacturers, *Transactions of Annual Meeting* (1906), p. 169.

10. *Ibid.,* p. 168; a similar sentiment is expressed in *Asia,* VI (March, 1906), 33.

11. *The Financial Age,* XIV (Nov. 19, 1906), 1187.

12. Resolution of the Boston Chamber of Commerce in the National Board of Trade, *Proceedings of the Thirty-eighth Annual Meeting* (1908), p. 47.

13. *Ibid., Proceedings of the Thirty-seventh Annual Meeting* (1907), p. 70.

14. *American Exporter,* LX (Aug. 1907), 3-4.

15. *Commercial and Financial Chronicle,* LXXXIV (Jan. 12, 1907), 69.

16. *The Banker's Magazine,* LXXV (Sept., 1907), 319-320.

17. *Commercial and Financial Chronicle,* LXXXV (Oct. 5, 1907), 832.

18. National Board of Trade, *Proceedings of the Thirty-eighth Annual Meeting* (1908), p. 265.

19. Chamber of Commerce of New York State, *Fifty-first Report* (1908-1909), p. 118.

20. Tupper and McReynolds, *op. cit.,* p. 68.

21. San Francisco, *Merchants' Association Review,* XII (March, 1909), 6.

22. John Hays Hammond, "American Commercial Interests in the Far East," *Annals of the American Academy of Political Science,* XXVI (July, 1905), 83-84.

23. Thomas F. Millard, *America and the Far Eastern Question* (New York, 1909), p. 150 ff.

24. *Ibid.,* p. 159-161.

25. Tupper and McReynolds, *op. cit.,* p. 83.

26. *Asia,* VI (June, 1906), 130; VI (Aug., 1906), 193-194.

27. *American Exporter-Domestic Supplement,* LXI (May, 1908), 3.

28. *American Exporter,* LVI (Sept., 1905), 93.

29. *Asia,* XI (June, 1911), 129-130.

30. New York *Journal of Commerce,* Feb. 14, 1908.

31. *Asia,* IX (April, 1909), 162.

32. New York *Journal of Commerce,* Dec. 1, 1908.

33. *New York Commercial,* Nov. 30, 1908.

34. Board of Trustees of the Chamber of Commerce of San Francisco, *Report of the Committee on Commercial Relations with Japan of the Honorary Commercial Commissioners Representing the Chambers of Commerce of the Pacific Coast of the United States of America on a Visit to Japan* (San Francisco, 1908), p. 40.

35. Lord Lindsay Russell, *America to Japan: A Symposium of Papers by Representative Citizens of the United States on the Relations between Japan and America on the Common Interests of the Two Countries* (New York, 1915).

36. Frederick V. Field, *American Participation in the Chinese Consortiums* (Chicago, 1931), p. 14.

37. *Asia*, IV (April, 1904), 88.

38. George Kennan, *Edward H. Harriman* (2 vols., New York, 1922), II, 2.

39. *Ibid.*, II, 1.

40. *Ibid.*, II 5-12.

41. The text of the agreement can be found in *Ibid.*, II, 14.

42. Komura cited Article VI of the Portsmouth Treaty as being inconsistent with the Harriman Memorandum. This article pledged Japan not to transfer the South Manchurian Railroad to anyone without the consent of the Chinese government. *Ibid.*, II, 16.

43. Willard Straight, "China's Loan Negotiations," in George H. Blakeslee, ed., *Recent Developments in China* (New York, 1913), p. 121.

44. Charles Vevier, *The United States in China, 1906-1913: A Study of Finance and Diplomacy* (New Brunswick, 1955), 46.

45. *Ibid.*, p. 48.

46. Herbert Croly, *Willard Straight* (New York, 1924), pp. 272-278.

47. Cyrus Adler, *Jacob Schiff — His Life and Letters* (2 vols., Garden City, 1928), II, pp. 248-250.

48. Croly, *op. cit.*, p. 279.

49. Vevier, *op. cit.*, pp. 98-108.

50. Field, *op. cit.*, pp. 21-24.

51. *Asia*, IX (July, 1909), 162.

52. *American Exporter-Domestic Supplement*, LXIV (July, 1909), 3-4.

53. Vevier, *op. cit.*, p. 163.

54. *Ibid.*, p. 149.

55. *Asia*, X (Sept., 1910), 225.

56. Vevier, *op. cit.*, p. 178.

57. For a detailed account of the difficulties that beset the International Consortium see Willard Straight in Blakesse, *op. cit.*, pp. 135-157.

58. The total value of American exports to China increased from $10,-405,834 in 1901 to $21,261,531. At the same time the value of all American exports increased from $1,487,764,991 to $2,428,506,358. U.S. Department of Commerce, *Statistical Abstracts of the United States*, 1913 (Washington, D.C., 1914), pp. 327 and 351.

4 | BUSINESS LOOKS AT LATIN AMERICA

1. John Hays Hammond, "The Development of Our Latin American Trade," in George H. Blakeslee, ed., *Latin America* (New York, 1914), p. 176.

72

2. National Association of Manufacturers, *Proceedings of the Fourteenth Annual Convention* (1909), p. 43.

3. *Iron Age,* LXV (April 5, 1900), 19.

4. *American Industries,* II (July 1, 1904), 5.

5. Hammond, *op. cit.,* p. 178.

6. *The Banker's Magazine,* LXXXIV (May, 1907), 700.

7. *Ibid.,* LXXXIV (March, 1907), 326.

8. United States Department of Commerce, *Statistical Abstracts of the United States,* 1913, pp. 339-41, 350.

9. Robert Dunn, *American Foreign Investments* (New York, 1926), pp. 2-3.

10. *Ibid.,* pp. 331-34.

11. *Senate Documents,* 60 Congress, 1 Sess. (1906), XXIV, No. 413, pp. 95-97.

12. Fred J. Rippy, *The Capitalists and Colombia* (New York, 1931), pp. 57-58.

13. Dunn, *op. cit.,* pp. 195-97.

14. F. C. Harrison and Charles Conant, *Monetary Reform for Nicaragua, Report Presenting a Plan of Monetary Reform for Nicaragua, Submitted to Messrs Brown Brothers and J. W. Seligman and Company* (New York, 1912), *passim.*

15. Charles David Kepner, Jr., and Jay Henry Soothill, *The Banana Empire: A Case Study of Economic Imperialism* (New York, 1935), p. 52.

16. *Ibid.,* p. 55.

17. U.S. Senate, Subcommittee of the Committee on Interstate Commerce, *Hearing on Resolution S. No. 139, Submitted by Mr. Johnston, Directing the Department of Commerce and Labor to Make An Investigation into the Character and Operations of the United Fruit Company,* Series No. 8, 60 Cong., 1 Sess. (April 22, 1908), pp. 3-14 *passium.*

18. National Association of Manufacturers, in Cooperation with Banking and Transportation Interests of the United States, *Proceedings of the International Trade Conference* (New York, 1915), p. 307.

19. Hammond, *op. cit.,* p. 178.

20. *Journal of Commerce and Commercial Bulletin* (New York), June 5, 1911.

21. New York and Bermudez Company, *The Seizure of the Property of the New York and Bermudez Company by the Venezulan Government: A Statement by the Company* (New York, 1906), pp. 1-57.

22. *Ibid.,* p. 22.

23. *Commercial and Financial Chronicle,* LXXV (Dec. 20, 1902), 1327.

24. *Bradstreet's,* XXXII (Feb. 17, 1904), 130.

25. *Ibid.,* XXXIII (March 25, 1905), 178.

26. *Commercial and Financial Chronicle,* LXXVI (Feb. 21, 1903), 405.

27. *American Banker,* LXVII (Jan. 4, 1902), 8.

28. *Marine Journal,* XXV (Feb. 7, 1903), 8.

29. Isaac Seligman, "International Banking and Its Important Influence on International Unity," *International Conciliation,* No. 50 (January, 1913), 24.

30. *Marine Journal,* XXVI (March 5, 1904), 3.

31. *New York Commercial, Santo Domingo, A Brief Sketch of the Island, Its Resources and Commercial Possibilities With Special Reference to the Treaty Now Pending in the United States Senate* (New York, 1906), pp. 2-33.

32. Philadelphia Board of Trade, *Seventy-Fourth Annual Report* (Philadelphia, 1907), p. 43.

33. *Wall Street Journal,* Jan. 18, 1907.

34. *American Exporter,* LXVI (Oct., 1910), 72.

35. *Protectionist,* XVI (March, 1905), 587.

36. *Commercial and Financial Chronicle,* LXXX (Jan. 28, 1904), 431.

37. *New York Commercial,* Dec. 4, 1908.

38. *American Exporter* (Domestic Supplement), LXV (Jan., 1910), 4.

39. *Protectionist,* XII (May, 1900), 24.

40. *Journal of Commerce,* editorial, reprinted in *ibid.* XV (Feb., 1904), 1279.

41. Charles Conant, "Our Duty in Cuba," *North American Review,* CLXXXV (May 13, 1907), 141-146.

42. *Journal of Commerce,* Oct. 15, 1908.

43. *The Financial Age,* XIV (Oct. 8, 1906), 769.

44. *Wall Street Journal,* Dec. 1, 1903.

45. *Protectionist,* XIII (May, 1901), 55.

5 | BUSINESS ATTITUDE TOWARD PEACE

1. Marcus A. Markes, address April 16, 1907, in the National Arbitration and Peace Congress, *Proceedings* (New York, 1907), p. 125.

2. James Van Clove, "Importance of Peace to Industry," speech April 16, 1907, in *ibid.,* pp. 128-39.

3. Sereno S. Pratt, "The Contribution of Commerce to International Unity," *International Conciliation,* No. 50 (Jan., 1912), 5.

4. *Wall Street Journal,* Feb. 14, 1907.

5. John Crosby Brown, "International Trade Leading to a Permanent Peace," speech May 29, 1902, in the Lake Mohonk Conference on International Arbitration, *Report of the Eighth Annual Meeting, 1902* (Lake Mohonk, New York, 1902), p. 69. This work will be hereafter cited as Lake Mohonk Conference, *Eighth Annual Meeting.*

6. Osborne Howes, "Trade, Treaties and Trusts as a Means of Allaying Animosities," speech May 29, 1902, in *ibid.,* p. 76.

7. Isaac M. Seligman, "International Banking and Its Important Influence on International Unity," *International Conciliation,* No. 50 (Jan., 1912), 21-22.

8. Henry Clews, "The Economies of Peace," *The Peace Forum,* II (May, 1914), 43, quoting *Trend.*

9. George L. Ridgeway, *Merchants of Peace, Twenty Years of Business Diplomacy Through the International Chamber of Commerce,* 1919-1938 (New York, 1938), p. 15.

10. *Protectionist,* XIX (June, 1907), 78-80.

11. George Foster Peabody, "Unreliability of Commercial Forces Working Alone," speech May 29, 1902, in Lake Mohonk Conference, *Eighth Annual Meeting,* 1902, p. 81.

12. Andrew Carnegie, *Address by Andrew Carnegie at Fourth American Peace Conference, St. Louis, 1913* (New York, 1913), p. 6.

13. A. B. Farquhar, speech June 2, 1904, in the Lake Mohonk Conference, *Report of the Tenth Annual Meeting* (Lake Mohonk, 1904), pp. 93-95.

14. Markes, *op. cit.,* p. 124.

15. Lake Mohonk Conference, *Report of the Ninth Annual Meeting, 1903,* p. 77.

16. *Commercial and Financial Chronicle,* LXXXI (Sept. 23, 1905), 942.

17. Henry Clews, "An Address Delivered at the Banquet Given in Honor of the President of the United States by the American Peace and Arbitration League," March 22, 1910 (New York, 1910).

18. Pratt, *op. cit.,* p. 10.

19. Lake Mohonk Conference, *Report of the Eighteenth Annual Conference,* 1912, p. 145.

20. *Ibid., Report of the Ninth Annual Conference* (Lake Mohonk, New York, 1903), p. 77.

21. National Board of Trade, *Proceedings of the Thirty-seventh Annual Meeting,* 1907, p. 66.

22. William F. King, "Commercial Aspects of International Arbitration," speech May 29, 1902, in Lake Mohonk Conference, *Report of the Eighth Annual Conference,* 1902, p. 71.

23. A. Foster Higgens, speech May 29, 1908, Lake Mohonk Conference, *Report of the Ninth Annual Conference,* 1903, p. 106.

24. New York *Journal of Commerce,* March 4, 1907.

25. "Chambers of Commerce for Arbitration," *World Peace Foundation Pamphlet Series,* No. 3, Part IV (Boston, 1911), p. 4.

26. Lake Mohonk Conference, *Report of the Eighteenth Annual Conference,* 1912, p. 151.

27. *The Banker's Magazine,* LXXI (Oct., 1905), 476-77.

28. A. B. Farquhar, "Outcome of the Second Hague Conference," speech May 21, 1908, in Lake Mohonk Conference, *Report of the Fourteenth Annual Meeting, 1908,* pp. 108-09.

29. National Board of Trade, *Proceedings of Thirty-seventh Annual Meeting, 1907,* p. 67.

30. "Information Desk," *The Peace Forum,* I (Oct., 1913), 21.

31. *Iron Age,* LXXXV (April 25, 1910), 998.

32. Henry Clews, "The Businessman's View," speech at Metropolitan Temple April 2, 1911, in *Peace,* I (Oct. 1912), 18.

33. *The Banker's Magazine,* LXXXIX (Sept., 1914), 212; *American Economist,* LIX (Aug. 7, 1914), 61.

34. *The New York Times,* Aug. 2, 1914.

35. From August through September, the moratorium on stock transactions imposed by the New York Stock Exchange seems to have been effective. By October, 1914, a clandestine trade in corporate securities had begun on New Street in the New York financial district. Records kept by several brokerage houses indicate that stock prices reached their low point around October 21. By the time the Exchange opened, stock prices had recovered to the level of July 30. *Commercial and Financial Chronicle,* XCIX (Dec. 26, 1914), 1865-6.

36. *Iron Age, XCIV* (Aug. 6, 1914), 354.

37. *Ibid.,* XCIV (Nov. 19, 1914), 1188.

38. *Manufacturers' Record,* LXVI (Aug. 13, 1914), 57.

39. *Ibid.,* LXVII (Jan. 14, 1915), 57.

40. *American Economist,* LV (June 11, 1915), 277.

41. *Iron Age,* XCIV (Oct. 29, 1914), 1035.

42. Bethlehem Steel rose from $29 to $275 a share and General Motors rose from $37 to $189 a share. *Commercial and Financial Chronicle,* CI (July 31, 1915), 318; CII (Jan. 29, 1916), 391; *Advocate of Peace,* LXXVII (May, 1916), 134.

43. Harold C. Syrett, "The Business Press and American Neutrality, 1914-1917," *The Mississippi Valley Historical Review,* XXXII (Sept., 1945), 215-230.

44. *Manufacturers Record,* LXVII (Jan. 28, 1915), 13.

45. *The Banker's Magazine,* XCI (Oct. 1915), 465; *Manufacturers Record,* LXVII (May 20, 1915), 39.

46. *Ibid.,* LXVIII (July 22, 1915), 33.

47. Lake Mohonk Conference, *Report of the Twenty-first Annual Conference, 1915,* p. 130.

48. *Commercial and Financial Chronicle,* C (Jan. 1, 1915), 19.

49. "Referendum on the Report of the Special Committee in the Economic Results of War on American business," *International Conciliation,* No. 77 (December, 1915), 9; Lake Mohonk Conference, *Report of the Twenty-second, 1916,* pp. 213-14.

50. Henry Ford, *My Life and Work* (Garden City, 1924), p. 246.

51. Allan Nevins and Frank Hill, *Ford: Expansion and Challenge 1915-1933* (New York, 1957), p. 26 ff; *Advocate of Peace,* LXXVIII (Jan., 1916), 28; *Commercial and Financial Chronicle,* CII (Feb. 3, 1916), 479.

52. *Ibid.,* CII (April 29, 1916), 1595.

53. *American Economist,* LIX (Sept. 18, 1914), 139; *Manufacturers Record,* LXVII (July 8, 1915), 33; *Commercial and Financial Chronicle,* XCIX (Oct. 17, 1914), 1096.

54. Lake Mohonk Conference, *Report of the Twenty-first Annual Conference, 1915,* p. 130.

55. *Commercial and Financial Chronicle,* XCIX (Dec. 15, 1914), 1638.

56. *Ibid.,* C (May 22, 1915), 1722.

57. *The Banker's Magazine,* XCII (May, 1916), 603.

58. *Manufacturers Record,* LXVIII (Aug. 19, 1915), 35.

59. Walter Millis, *Road to War: America, 1914-1917* (Boston, 1935); Charles C. Tansill, *America Goes to War* (Boston, 1938).

60. *The Banker's Magazine,* XCIII (December, 1916), 515-516; 579-580.

61. Syrett, *op. cit.,* p. 223.

6582 Ш

DATE DUE

2-27-70			
GAYLORD			PRINTED IN U.S.A.